The Thomas D. Clark Lectures

1993

FAIRY TALE AS MYTH

MYTH AS FAIRY TALE

Jack Zipes

THE UNIVERSITY PRESS OF KENTUCKY

Publication of this book was assisted by a grant from the Gaines Center for the Humanities, which initiated and supports the Thomas D. Clark Lectureship Series.

Scholarly publisher for the Commonwealth, serving Bellarmine College, Berea College, Centre College of Kentucky, Eastern Kentucky University, The Filson Club, Georgetown College, Kentucky Historical Society, Kentucky State University, Morehead State University, Murray State University, Northern Kentucky University, Transylvania University, University of Kentucky, University of Louisville, and Western Kentucky University.

Editorial and Sales Offices: The University Press of Kentucky 663 South Limestone Street, Lexington, Kentucky 40508-4008

Permission has been granted by the publishers to reprint the following essays in revised form: "The Origins of the Fairy Tale or, How Script Was Used to Tame the Beast in Us," in *Children and Their Books*, ed. Gillian Avery and Julia Briggs (Oxford: Oxford Univ. Press, 1989), 119-34; "Spreading Myths about Fairy Tales: A Critical Commentary on Robert Bly's *Iron John*," *New German Critique* 55 (Winter 1992): 3-20; "Recent Trends in the Contemporary American Fairy Tale," *Journal of the Fantastic in the Arts* 5 (1992): 13-41; "Spinning with Fate: Rumplestiltskin and the Decline of Female Productivity," *Journal of Western Folklore* 52 (January 1993): 43-60.

Library of Congress Cataloging-in-Publication Data

Zipes, Jack David.
    Fairy tale as myth/myth as fairy tale / Jack Zipes.
        p.   cm. — (The Thomas D. Clark lectures : 1993)
    Includes bibliographical references and index.
    ISBN 0-8131-1890-5. —ISBN 0-8131-0834-9 (pbk.)
    1. Fairy tales—History and criticism. 2. Fairy tales—Classification. I. Title.
GR550.Z56 1994
398.21—dc20   94-13777

This book is printed on acid-free recycled paper meeting the requirements of the American National Standard for Permanence of Paper for Printed Library Materials.

Manufactured in the United States of America

FOR

Judy Pasamanick and Catherine Velay-Vallantin
who have inspired my work
on both sides of the ocean

CONTENTS

ILLUSTRATIONS

ACKNOWLEDGMENTS

In preparing this book for publication I have received invaluable support from friends and colleagues. In particular, Cristina Bacchilega and Steven Swann Jones provided many necessary corrections in my critique of folklore scholarship in the Rumpelstiltskin chapter, and Ruth-Ellen Joeres was most helpful in refining my feminist perspective. Linda and Jochen Schulte-Sasse offered sound advice about my notion of violation in the introduction and in the Disney chapter and urged me to consider modernism and technology in a more balanced way than my original draft presented. Elizabeth Bell also helped me revise several questionable assertions in this chapter. Some of these chapters were first published as essays in *New German Critique*, *Journal of the Fantastic in the Arts*, *Journal of Western Folklore*, and *Children and Their Books* and have been extensively revised for this book. Some were presented at conferences such as the lively one held by the International Association for the Fantastic in the Arts or at various universities, and I benefited from the questions and critical points raised by numerous people in discussion sessions. In particular I am very much indebted to Jeannine Blackwell, who invited me to deliver three Thomas D. Clark lectures at the University of Kentucky during the fall of 1993. Thanks to her prompting, I was able to rework my lectures and manuscripts for publication.

There are always questions when one talks or writes on fairy tales that can never be totally answered, for they touch our lives in deep and mysterious ways, but I do hope that this book may respond effectively to some of the crucial questions that pertain to the mythical workings of the fairy tale in our own day.

INTRODUCTION

Attached, almost as an afterthought, to the end of Mircea Eliade's book *Myth and Reality*[1] is a highly stimulating essay entitled "Myths and Fairy Tales." First published as a review of a book that dealt with the relationship of the fairy tale to the heroic legend and myth,[2] Eliade's essay was concerned not only with demonstrating the differences between myth and fairy tale but also with elaborating their extraordinary symbiotic connection.

It is well known that Eliade, one of the great scholars of religion and myth, believed that "myth narrates a sacred history; it relates an event that took place in primordial Time, the fabled time of the 'beginnings.' In other words, myth tells us how, through the deeds of Supernatural Beings, a reality came into existence, be it the whole of reality, the Cosmos, or only a fragment of reality—an island, a species of plant, a particular kind of human behavior, an institution."[3] Since myth narrates the deeds of supernatural beings, it sets examples for human beings that enable them to codify and order their lives. By enacting and incorporating myths in their daily lives, humans are able to have a genuine religious experience. Indeed, it is through recalling and bringing back the gods of the past into the present that one becomes their contemporary and at the same time is transported into primordial or sacred time. This transportation is also a connection, for a mortal can gain a sense of his or her origins and feel the process of history in the present and time as divine.

In contrast to the myth—and here Eliade often conflates the genre of the oral folk tale with the literary fairy tale—he argues that "we never find in folk tales an accurate memory of a particular stage of culture; cultural styles and historical cycles are telescoped in them. All that remains is the structure of an exemplary behavior."[4] However, this does not mean that oral folk tales and literary fairy tales are desacralized narratives. On the contrary—and this is Eliade's important point—they continue to convey mythic notions and motifs that are camouflaged. In one key passage of his essay, Eliade states that, "though in the West the tale has long since become a literature of diversion (for children and peasants) or of escape (for city dwellers), it still presents the structure of an infinitely serious and responsible adventure, for in the last analysis it is reducible to an initiatory scenario: again and again we find initiatory ordeals (battles with the monster, apparently insurmountable obstacles, riddles to be solved, impossible tasks, etc.), the descent to Hades or the ascent to Heaven (or—what amounts to the same thing—death and resurrection), marrying the princess."[5] All of this becomes camouflaged, according to Eliade, when the tale abandons its clear religious "initiatory" responsibility, but appropriates the scenario and certain motifs, and one of the intriguing questions for folklorists and those scholars interested in myths and fairy tales is to determine why and when all this took place.

Eliade believes it may have occurred when the traditional rites and secrets of cults were no longer practiced and when it was no longer taboo to reveal and tell the "mysteries" of the religious practices. Whatever the case may be, it is clear to Eliade that the myth preceded the folk and fairy tale and that it had a more sacred function in communities and societies than the secular narratives.

Of course, there have been great debates among scholars about whether the myth preceded the oral folk tale and whether it is a higher form of art because it encompasses the religious experience of people. But this debate is not what interests me with regard to Eliade's essay, rather it is the manner in which he almost equates the religious myth with the secular fairy tale. That is, he tends to regard the folk tale as the profane conveyor of the religious experience. "The tale takes up and continues 'initiation' on the level of the imaginary," he says. "All unwittingly, and indeed believing that he is merely amusing himself or escaping, the man of modern societies still benefits from the imaginary initiation supplied by tales. That being so, one may wonder if the fairy tale did not very early become an 'easy doublet' for the initiation myth and rites, if it did not have the role of re-creating the 'initiatory ordeals' on the plane of imagination and dream."[6]

The fairy tale or, to be more specific, the folk tale, as an "easy doublet for the initiation myth." That is an astonishing idea. It could mean that, from the beginning, individual imaginations were countering the codified myths of a tribe or society that celebrated the power of gods with other "non-authoritative" tales of their own that called upon and transformed the supernatural into magical and mysterious forces which could change their lives. Certainly, myths and folk tales blended very early in the oral tradition, and in many modern oral and literary narratives it is very difficult to tell them apart. They seem to be invested with an extraordinary mystical power so that we collapse the distinctions and feel compelled to return to them time and again for counsel and guidance, for hope that there is some divine order and sense to a chaotic world.

Myths and fairy tales seem to know something that we do not know. They also appear to hold our attention, to keep us in their sway, to enchant our lives. We keep returning to them for answers. We use them in diverse ways as private sacred myths or as public commercial advertisements to sell something. We refer to myths and fairy tales as lies by saying, "oh, that's just a fairy tale," or "that's just myth." But these lies are often the lies that govern our lives.

Over the centuries we have transformed the ancient myths and folk tales and made them into the fabric of our lives. Consciously and unconsciously we weave the narratives of myth and folk tale into our daily existence. During one period in our history, the Enlightenment, it seemed that we people of reason were about to disenchant the world and get rid of all the old myths and religions that enfeebled our minds so that we could see clearly and act rationally to create a world of equality and liberty. But, as Theodor Adorno and Max Horkheimer noted in their most significant contribution to critical theory, *Dialectic of Enlightenment*, we simply replaced archaic myths with a new myth of our own based on the conviction that our own civilized reason had the true power to improve the living and working conditions of all human beings; it was not the power of the gods that would help humankind. It was the rising bourgeoisie that spoke out in the name of all human beings while really speaking in its own interests, and these interests are the myths that pervade our lives today.

But these myths are not new, nor are they just myths, for they are also fairy tales. These myths and fairy tales are historically and culturally coded, and their ideological impact is great. Somehow they have become codified, authoritative, and canonical. We talk of classical myths and classical fairy tales. They seem to have been with us for centuries, for eternity, but we neglect the manner in which we created gods and magic to hold our experiences and lives intact.

Perhaps that is "natural." I mean we need standards, order, models. As Freud pointed out in *Civilization and Its Discontents*, culture cannot exist without repression and sublimation, and it is within the civilizing process that we establish the rules by which we live. We seek to make these rules stick and become eternal. We classify and categorize to establish types and values. We weed out, modify, and purify, seeking the classical statement or form. We want to make our lives classic, and we construe roles for ourselves through classical models and narratives. They are all around us in Barbie dolls and fairy tales.

When we think of the fairy tale today, we primarily think of the classical fairy tale. We think of those fairy tales that are the most popular in the western world: *Cinderella, Snow White, Little Red Riding Hood, Sleeping Beauty, Rapunzel, Beauty and the Beast, Rumpelstiltskin, The Ugly Duckling, The Princess and the Pea, Puss in Boots, The Frog King, Jack and the Beanstalk, Tom Thumb, The Little Mermaid.* It is *natural* to think mainly of these fairy tales as if they had always been with us, as if they were part of our nature. Newly written fairy tales, especially those that are innovative and radical, are unusual, exceptional, strange, and artificial because they do not conform to the patterns set by the classical fairy tale. And, if they do conform and become familiar, we tend to forget them after a while, because the classical fairy tale suffices. We are safe with the familiar. We shun the new, the real innovations. The classical fairy tale makes it appear that we are all part of a universal community with shared values and norms, that we are all striving for the same happiness, that there are certain dreams and wishes which are irrefutable, that a particular type of behavior will produce guaranteed results, like living happily ever after with lots of gold in a marvelous castle, *our* castle and fortress that will forever protect us from inimical and unpredictable forces of the outside world. We need only have faith and believe in the classical fairy tale, just as we are expected to have faith and believe in the American flag as we swear the pledge of allegiance.

The fairy tale is myth. That is, the classical fairy tale has undergone a process of mythicization. Any fairy tale in our society, if it seeks to become natural and eternal, must become myth. Only innovative fairy tales are antimythical, resist the tide of mythicization, comment on the fairy tale as myth. Even the classical myths are no longer valid as Myths with a capital M. That is, the classical myths have also become ideologically mythicized, dehistoricized, depoliticized to represent and maintain the hegemonic interests of the bourgeoisie. Classical myths and fairy tales are contemporary myths that pervade our daily lives in the manner described by Roland Barthes in *Mythologies*[7] and in *Image—Music—Text*.[8] For Barthes, myth is a collective representation that is socially determined and then inverted so as not to appear as a cultural artefact. "Myth consists in overturning culture into nature or, at least, the social, the cultural, the ideological, the historical into the 'natural'. What is nothing but a product of class division and its moral, cultural and aesthetic consequences is presented (stated) as being a 'matter of course'; under the effect of mythical inversion, the quite contingent foundations of the utterance become Common Sense, Right Reason, the Norm, General Opinion, in short the *doxa* (which is the secular figure of the Origin)."[9]

As a message and type of verbal or visual speech, contemporary myth is derived from a semiological system that has undergone and continues to undergo a historical-political development. Paradoxically the myth acts to deny its historical and systematic development. It takes material that already has a signification and reworks it parasitically to make it suitable for communication in an ideological mode that appears nonideological. Barthes argues that "myth is a double system; there occurs in it a sort of ubiquity: its point of departure is constituted by the arrival of a meaning."[10] Essentially, it is the concept behind the formation of the myth that endows it with a value or signification so that the form of the myth is totally at the service of the concept. Myth is manipulated speech. Or, as Barthes defines it, "myth is a type of speech defined by its intention . . . much more than by its literal sense . . . and in spite of this, its intention is somehow frozen, purified, eternalized, *made absent* by this literal sense."[11] As frozen speech, "myth suspends itself, turns away and assumes the look of a generality: it stiffens, it makes itself look neutral and innocent. . . . On the surface of language something has stopped moving: the use of the signification is here, hiding behind the fact, and conferring on it a notifying look; but at the same time, the fact paralyses the intention, gives it something like a malaise producing immobility: in order to make it innocent, it freezes it. This is because myth is speech *stolen and restored*. Only, speech which is restored is no longer quite that which was stolen: when it was brought back, it was not put exactly in its place. It is this brief act of larceny, this moment taken for a surreptitious faking, which gives mythical speech its benumbed look."[12]

The fairy tale, which has become the mythified classical fairy tale, is indeed petrified in its restored constellation: it is a stolen and frozen cultural good, or *Kulturgut* as the Germans might say. What belonged to archaic societies, what belonged to pagan tribes and communities was passed down by word of mouth as a good only to be hardened into script, Christian and patriarchal. It has undergone and undergoes a motivated process of revision, reordering, and refinement. All the tools of modern industrial society (the printing press, the radio, the camera, the film, the record, the videocassette) have made their mark on the fairy tale to make it classical ultimately in the name of the bourgeoisie which refuses to be named, denies involvement; for the fairy tale must appear harmless, natural, eternal, ahistorical, therapeutic. We are to live and breate the classical fairy tale as fresh, free air. We are led to believe that this air has not been contaminated and polluted by a social class that will not name itself, wants us to continue believing that all air is fresh and free, all fairy tales spring from thin air.

Obviously, we cannot trace the "real" origins of fairy tales to their roots. But we can gain a sense of their historical transformation as genre and how they become mythified or are associated with myths in different historical periods.

What interests me most in this book is the manner in which the fairy tale as genre sets parameters for a discourse of the mores, values, gender, and power in the civilizing process and how the parameters and individual tales are frozen or become standardized, only to be subverted in a process of duplication and revision. Here it is important to define what I mean by duplication and revision.

The world *duplication* has three major meanings: it is (1) the act of doubling something; (2) the repetition of an action or thing; (3) the folding of something in two. Implicit in these meanings is that the part which is made from the other is exactly the same, or, at least, corresponds to it almost exactly. In other words, one part should be able to pass for the other so that the unsuspecting viewer might not be able to distinguish which part is the original. However, as we all know, most copies are generally discernible because it is practically impossible to duplicate anything exactly as it is. This fact is not disturbing because most people do not demand exact copies to possess *the original*; rather they want copies for proof, evidence, remembrance or because they are fond of something they cannot possess. A duplicate is not an original; it is a representation that attests to the fact that there is an original. The duplicate mimics the original; it is not unique, creative, or stimulating. It is there to dupe us, deceive us, dope us so that we do not have to recreate the original ourselves. It saves our mind energy by providing a near facsimile of what we have seen, read, or heard. It recalls patterns and repeats them in a familiar way so that we are deluded and believe that the copy is almost as good as the original. It enables us to fall back on the comfortable familiar object that does not challenge our customary routines or habits. The duplicate reinforces the deeply entrenched modes of thinking, conceiving, believing that provide our lives with structure. Since the conditions of life change so rapidly, we need to hold on to what we know and like quickly before it vanishes. So we copy. We duplicate.

We live in an age of mechanical reproduction where there are more copies of original art works than there are originals. We copy others in the way we dress, buy, and desire. We desire through the constant repetition of commercials that we copy whenever we shape ourselves and consume. To copy somebody else or something is to become a look-alike and make a coded statement.

To copy a fairy tale is to duplicate its message and images, to produce a look-alike. To duplicate a *classical* fairy tale is to reproduce a set pattern of ideas and images that reinforce a traditional way of seeing, believing, and behaving. It does not take much imagination or skill to duplicate a classical fairy tale. Nor is it expensive for publishers to print duplicates. The text is not copyrighted, and the illustrations correspond to a fixed pattern that has rarely been altered in their history of reproduction. The purpose for the publisher is to make money by reproducing staple products that will sell. The consumers/viewers want comfort and pleasure: they are not threatened, challenged, excited, or shocked by the duplications. A traditional and socially conservative world view is confirmed.

Revisions of classical fairy tales are different. According to the *Oxford Universal Dictionary*, *revise* means "To look or read carefully over, with a view to improving or correcting 1611," "To go over again, re-examine, in order to improve or amend."[13] The purpose of producing a revised fairy tale is to create something new that incorporates the critical and creative thinking of the producer and corresponds to changed demands and tastes of audiences. As a result of transformed values, the revised classical fairy tale seeks to alter the reader's views of traditional patterns, images, and codes. This does not mean that all revised classical fairy tales are improvements and progressive. Revision for the sake of revision is not necessarily a change for the better or stimulating. However, the premise of a revision is that there is something wrong with an original work and that it needs to be changed for the better. Qualitative transformation is of essence in a revision, whereas duplication is more concerned with maintaining whatever value was contained in the original. In fact, quality does not play much of a role in duplication because it does not demand a critical reexamination of the original work.

It is impossible to grasp the history of the fairy tale and the relationship of the fairy tale to myth without taking into consideration the manner in which tales have been revised and duplicated. To be more precise, the evolution of the fairy tale as a literary genre is marked by a process of dialectical appropriation involving duplication and revision that set the cultural conditions for its mythicization, institutionalization, and expansion as a mass-mediated form through radio, film, and television. Fairy tales were first *told* by gifted tellers and were based on rituals intended to endow meaning to the daily lives of members of a tribe. As *oral folk tales*, they were intended to explain natural occurrences such as the change of the seasons and shifts in the weather or to celebrate the rites of harvesting, hunting, marriage, and conquest. The emphasis in most folk tales was on communal harmony. A narrator or narrators told tales to bring members of a group or tribe closer together and to provide them with a sense of mission, a telos. The tales themselves assumed a generic quality based on the function that they were to fulfill for the community or the incidents that they were to report, describe, and explain. Consequently, there were tales of initiation, worship, warning, and indoctrination. Whatever the type may have been, the voice of the narrator was known. The tale came directly from common experiences and beliefs. Told in person, directly, fact to face, they were altered as the beliefs and behaviors of the members of a particular group changed.

With the rise of literacy and the invention of the printing press in the fifteenth century, the oral tradition of storytelling underwent an immense revolution. The oral tales were taken over by a different social class, and the form, themes, production, and reception of the tales were transformed. This change did not happen overnight, but it did foster discrimination among writers and their audiences almost immediately so that distinct genres were recognized and approved for certain occasions and functions within polite society or cultivated circles of readers. In the case of folk tales, they were gradually categorized as legends, myths, fables, comical anecdotes, and, of course, fairy tales.

What we today consider fairy tales were actually just one type of the folk-tale tradition, namely the *Zaubermärchen* or the magic tale, which has many subgenres. The French writers of the late seventeenth century called these tales *contes de fées* (fairy tales) to distinguish them from other kinds of *contes populaires* (popular tales), and what really distinguished a *conte de fée,* based on the oral *Zaubermärchen,* was its transformation into a literary tale that addressed the concerns, tastes, and functions of court society. The fairy tale had to fit into the French salons, parlors, and courts of the aristocracy and bourgeoisie if it was to establish itself as a genre. The writers, Madame D'Aulnoy, Charles Perrault, Mademoiselle L'Héritier, Mademoiselle de La Force, and many others knew and expanded upon oral and literary tales. They were not, however, the initiators of the literary fairy-tale tradition in Europe.[14] Two Italian writers, Giovanni Francesco Straparola and Giambattista Basile, had already set an example for what the French were accomplishing.[15] But the French writers created an institution; that is, the genre of the literary fairy tale was institutionalized as an aesthetic and social means through which questions and issues of civilité, proper behavior and demeanor in all types of situations, were mapped out as narrative strategies for literary socialization, and in many cases, as symbolical gestures of subversion to question the ruling standards of taste and behavior.

While the literary fairy tale was being institutionalized at the end of the seventeenth century and beginning of the eighteenth century in France, the oral tradition did not disappear, nor was it subsumed by the new literary genre. Rather, the oral tradition continued to feed the writers with material and was now also influenced by the literary tradition itself. The early chapbooks or (cheap books) that were carried by peddlers or *colporteurs* to the villages throughout France known as the *Bibliothéque Bleue* contained numerous abbreviated and truncated versions of the literary tales, and these were in turn told once again in these communities. In some cases, the literary tales presented new material that was transformed through the oral tradition and returned later to literature by a writer who remembered hearing a particular story.

By the beginning of the nineteenth century when the Brothers Grimm set about to celebrate German culture through their country's folk tales, the literary fairy tale had long since been institutionalized, and they, along with Hans Christian Andersen, Collodi, Ludwig Bechstein, and a host of Victorian writers from George MacDonald to Oscar Wilde, assumed different ideological and aesthetic positions within this institutionalization. These writers put the finishing touches on the fairy-tale genre at a time when nation-states were assuming their modern form and cultivating particular forms of literature as commensurate expressions of national cultures.

What were the major prescriptions, expectations, and standards of the literary fairy tale by the end of the nineteenth century?

Here it is important first to make some general remarks about the "violent" shift from the oral to the literary tradition and not just talk about the appropriation of the magic folk tale as a dialectical process. Appropriation does not occur without violence to the rhetorical text created in the oral tales.[16] Such violation of oral storytelling was crucial and necessary for the establishment of the bourgeoisie because it concerned the control of desire and imagination within the symbolical order of western culture.

Unlike the oral tradition, the literary tale was written down to be read in private, although, in some cases, the fairy tales were read aloud in parlors. However, the book form enabled the reader to withdraw from his or her society and to be alone with a tale. This privatization violated the communal aspects of the folk tale, but the very printing of a fairy tale was already a violation since it was based on separation of social classes. Extremely few people could read, and the fairy tale in form and content furthered notions of elitism and separation. In fact, the French fairy tales heightened the aspect of the chosen aristocratic elite who were always placed at the center of the seventeenth and eighteenth century narratives. They were part and parcel of the class struggles in the discourses of that period. To a certain extent, the fairy tales were the outcome of violent "civilized" struggles, material representations of struggles for hegemony. As Nancy Armstrong and Leonard Tennenhouse have suggested, "a class of people cannot produce themselves as a ruling class without setting themselves off against certain Others. Their hegemony entails possession of the key cultural terms determining what are the right and wrong ways to be a human being." [17] No matter where the literary tale took root and established itself—France, Germany, England—it was written in a standard "high" language that the folk could not read, and it was written as a form of entertainment and education for members of the ruling classes. Indeed, only the well-to-do could purchase the books and read them. In short, by institutionalizing the literary fairy tale, writers and publishers violated the forms and concerns of nonliterate, essentially peasant communities and set new standards of taste, production, and reception through the discourse of the fairy tale.

The literary fairy tales tended to exclude the majority of people who could not read while the folk tales were open to everyone. Indeed, the literary narratives were individualistic

and unique in form and exalted the power of those chosen
to rule. In contrast, the oral tales had themes and characters
that were readily recognizable and reflected common wish-
fulfillments. Of course, one had to know the dialect in
which they were told. From a philological standpoint, the
literary fairy tale elevated the oral tale through the standard
practice of printing and setting grammatical rules in "high
French" or "high German." The process of violation is *not*
one of total negation and should not be studied as one-
dimensional, for the print culture enabled the tales to be
preserved and cultivated, and the texts created a new realm
of pleasurable reading that allowed for greater reflection on
the part of the reader than an oral performance of a tale
could do. At the beginning, the literary fairy tales were written and published for adults, and though they were intended
to reinforce the mores and values of French civilité, they were
so symbolical and could be read on so many different levels
that they were considered somewhat dangerous: social behavior could not be totally dictated, prescribed, and con-
trolled through the fairy tale, and there were subversive features in language and theme. This is one of the reasons that
fairy tales were not particularly approved for children. In
most European countries it was not until the end of the eighteenth and early part of the nineteenth centuries that fairy
tales were published for children, and even then begrudg-
ingly, because their "vulgar" origins in the lower classes were
suspect.

Of course, the fairy tales for children were sanitized and
expurgated versions of the fairy tales for adults, or they
were new moralistic tales that were aimed at the domestication of the imagination, as Rüdiger Steinlein has demonstrated in his significant study.[18] The form and structure of
the fairy tale for children were carefully regulated in the
nineteenth century so that improper thoughts and ideas
would not be stimulated in the minds of the young. If one
looks carefully at the major writers of fairy tales for chil-

dren who became classical and popular in the nineteenth century,[19] it is clear that they themselves exercised self-censorship and restraint in conceiving and writing down tales for children.

This is not to argue that the literary fairy tale as institution became one in which the imagination was totally domesticated. On the contrary, by the end of the nineteenth century the genre served different functions. As a whole, it formed a multi-vocal network of discourses through which writers used familiar motifs, topoi, protagonists, and plots symbolically to comment on the civilizing process and socialization in their respective countries. These tales did not represent communal values but rather the values of a particular writer. Therefore, if the writer subscribed to the hegemonic value system of his or her society and respected the canonical ideology of Perrault, the Grimms, and Andersen, he/she would write a conventional tale with conservative values, whether for adults or children. On the other hand, many writers would parody, mock, question, and undermine the classical literary tradition and produce original and subversive tales that were part and parcel of the institution itself.

The so-called original and subversive tales kept and keep the dynamic quality of the dialectical appropriation alive, for there was and is always a danger that the written word, in contrast to the spoken word, will fix a structure, image, metaphor, plot, and value as sacrosanct, thereby lending it mythic proportions. For instance, for some people the Grimms' fairy tales are holy, or fairy tales are considered holy and not to be touched. How did this notion emanate?

To a certain extent it was engendered by the Grimms and other folklorists who believed that the fairy tales arose from the spirit of the folk and were related to myth. Yet, worship of the fairy tale as holy scripture is more of a petrification of the fairy tale that is connected to the establishment of correct speech, values, and power more than anything else.

This establishment through the violation of the oral practices was the great revolution and transformation of the
fairy tale, and led to mythicization of key classical fairy
tales. It is the fairy tale as myth that has extraordinary power in our daily lives, and its guises are manifold, its transformations astonishing. We often forget or are unaware of how
"mythic" and "changeable" fairy tales are. This book seeks
to explore why we ignore and yet are captivated by the fairy
tale as myth and the myth as fairy tale.

1. THE ORIGINS OF THE FAIRY TALE

In his endeavor to establish the origins of the fairy tale for children, Peter Brooks stated that "when at the end of the seventeenth century Perrault writes down and publishes tales which had been told for indeterminate centuries—and would continue to be told, and would be collected in varying versions by the Grimm Brothers and other modern folklorists—he seems to be performing for children's literature what must have been effected for *literature* long before: that is, he is creating a literature where before there had been myth and folklore. The act of transcription, both creative and destructive, takes us from the primitive to the modern, makes the stories and their themes enter into literacy, into civilization, into history."[1] Indeed, almost all literary historians tend to agree with Brooks that the point of origin of the literary fairy tale for children is with Charles Perrault's *Contes du temps passé* (1697);[2] yet they never adequately explain why this came about in relation to the development of *civilité*[3] and place too much emphasis on Perrault and his one volume of tales. Indeed, Perrault never intended his book to be read by children but was more concerned with demonstrating how French folklore could be adapted to the tastes of French high culture and used as a new genre of art within the French civilizing process. And Perrault was not alone in this "mission."

In order to comprehend the historical origin of the liter-

Illustration by Walter Crane, 1875.

ary fairy tale for children *and* adults in France toward the
end of the seventeenth century, we must shift the focus away
from one author and try to grasp how many authors contributed to the formation of the literary fairy tale as *institution*. It was not Perrault but groups of writers, particularly
aristocratic women, who gathered in salons during the seventeenth century and created the conditions for the rise of
the fairy tale. They set the groundwork for the institutionalization of the fairy tale as a "proper" genre intended first
for educated adult audiences and only later for children
who were to be educated according to a code of *civilité* that
was being elaborated in the seventeenth and eighteenth centuries. But what does institutionalization of the fairy tale
mean? What were the conditions during the seventeenth
century that led aristocratic women for the most part to
give birth, so to speak, to the literary fairy tale? These ques-

tions are important to address, if we want to understand our contemporary attitudes toward fairy tales and their seemingly universal appeal. As we shall see, their "universality" has more to do with the specific manner in which they were constructed historically as mythic constellations than with common psychic processes of a collective unconscious. Literary fairy tales are socially symbolical acts and narrative strategies formed to take part in civilized discourses about morality and behavior in particular societies and cultures. They are constantly rearranged and transformed to suit changes in tastes and values, and they assume mythic proportions when they are frozen in an ideological constellation that makes it seem that there are universal absolutes that are divine and should not be changed. To clarify how the mythization of fairy tales evolved, I propose to discuss first the significance of the institutionalization of the fairy tale and then to analyze how *Beauty and the Beast* has assumed mythic features during the past three hundred years.

The importance of the term "institutionalization" for studying the origins of the literary fairy tale can best be understood if we turn to Peter Bürger's *Theory of the Avant-Garde*.[4] Bürger argues that "works of art are not received as single entities, but within institutional frameworks and conditions that largely determine the function of the works. When one refers to the function of an individual work, one generally speaks figuratively; for the consequences that one may observe or infer are not primarily a function of its special qualities but rather of the manner which regulates the commerce with works of this kind in a given society or in certain strata or classes of a society. I have chosen the term 'institution of art' to characterize such framing conditions."[5]

The framing conditions that constitute the institution of art (which includes literature in the broad sense) are the purpose or function, production, and reception. For instance, Bürger divides the development of art from the late Middle Ages to the present into the following phases:[6]

	Sacral Art	*Courtly Art*	*Bourgeois Art*
Function or	cult object	representational	portrayal of
Purpose		object	bourgeois self-
			understanding
Production	collective	individual	individual
	craft		
Reception	collective	collective	individual
	(sacral)	(sociable)	

In the period that concerns us, art at the court of Louis XIV, Bürger maintains that art is "representational and serves the glory of the prince and the self-portrayal of courtly society. Courtly art is part of the life praxis of courtly society, just as sacral art is part of the life praxis of the faithful. Yet the detachment from the sacral tie is a first step in the emancipation of art. ('Emancipation' is being used here as a descriptive term, as referring to the process by which art constitutes itself as a distinct social subsystem.) The difference from sacral art becomes particularly apparent in the realm of production: the artist produces as an individual and develops a consciousness of the uniqueness of his activity. Reception, on the other hand, remains collective. But the content of the collective performance is no longer sacral, it is socialibility."[7]

If we examine the rise of the literary fairy tale during the seventeenth century in light of Bürger's notion of institution, we can make the following observations. The literary fairy tale was first developed in salons by aristocratic women as a type of parlor game by the middle of the seventeenth century.[8] It was within the aristocratic salons that women were able to demonstrate their intelligence and education through different types of conversational games. In fact, the linguistic games often served as models for literary genres such as the occasional lyric or the serial novel. Both women and men participated in these games and were constantly challenged to invent new ones or to refine the games. Such

challenges led the women, in particular, to improve the
quality of their dialogues, remarks, and ideas about morals,
manners, and education and at times to oppose male standards that have been set to govern their lives. The subject
matter of the conversations consisted of literature, mores,
taste, and etiquette, whereby the speakers all endeavored to
portray ideal situations in the most effective oratorical style
that would gradually have a major effect on literary forms.

In the case of the literary fairy tale, though one cannot
fix the exact date that it became an acceptable game, we
know that there are various references to it toward the end
of the seventeenth century and that it emanated out of the
"jeux d'esprit" in the salons. The women would refer to
folk tales and use certain motifs spontaneously in their conversations. Eventually, women began telling the tales as a
literary divertimento, intermezzo, or as a kind of dessert
that one would invent to amuse other listeners. This social
function of amusement was complemented by another purpose, namely, that of self-portrayal and representation of
proper aristocratic manners. The telling of fairy tales enabled women to picture themselves, social manners, and relations in a manner that represented their interests and
those of the aristocracy. Thus, they placed great emphasis
on certain rules of oration such as naturalness and form-
lessness. The teller of the tale was to make it "seem" as
though the tale were made up on the spot and did not follow prescribed rules. Embellishment, improvisation, and
experimentation with known folk or literary motifs were
stressed. The procedure of telling a tale as "bagatelle" would
work as follows: the narrator would be requested to think
up a tale based on a particular motif; the adroitness of the
narrator would be measured by the degree with which
she/he was inventive and natural; the audience would respond politely with a compliment; then another member of
the audience would be requested to tell a tale, not in direct
competition with the other teller, but in order to continue

the game and vary the possibilities for linguistic expression.

By the 1690s the salon fairy tale became so acceptable that women and men began writing their tales down to publish them. The most notable writers gathered in the salons or homes of Madame D'Aulnoy, Perrault, Madame de Murat, Mademoiselle L'Héritier, or Mademoiselle de La Force, all of whom were in some part responsible for the great mode of literary fairy tales that developed between 1697 and 1789 in France.[9] The aesthetics developed in the conversational games and in the written tales had a serious side: though the tales differed in style and content, they were all anticlassical and were implicitly told and written in opposition to Nicolas Boileau, who was championing Greek and Roman literature as the models for French writers to follow at that time.[10] In addition, since the majority of the writers and tellers of fairy tales were women, there is a definite distinction to be made between their tales and those written and told by men. As Renate Baader has commented:

While Perrault's bourgeois and male tales with happy ends had pledged themselves to a moral that called for Griseldis to serve as a model for women, the women writers had to make an effort to defend the insights that had been gained in the past decades. Mlle Scudéry's novels and novellas stood as examples for them and taught them how to redeem their own wish reality in the fairy tale. They probably remembered how feminine faults had been revalorized by men and how the aristocratic women had responded to this in their self-portraits. Those aristocratic women had commonly refused to place themselves in the service of social mobility. Instead they put forward their demand for moral, intellectual, and psychological self-determination. As an analogy to this, the fairy tales of the women made it expected that the imagination in the tales was truly to be let loose in any kind of arbitrary way that had been considered a female danger up until that time. After the utopia of the "royaume de tendre," which had tied fairy-tale salvation of the sexes to a previous ascetic and enlightened practice of virtues and the guidance of feelings, there was now an unleashed imagination that could invent a fairy-tale realm and embellish it so that reason and will were set out of commission.[11]

If we were to take the major literary fairy tales produced at the end of the seventeenth century—Madame D'Aulnoy, *Les Contes des Fées* (1697-98), Mademoiselle La Force, *Les Contes des Contes* (1697), Mademoiselle L'Héritier, *Oeuvres meslées* (1696), Chevalier de Mailly, *Les Illustres Féés* (1698), Madame de Murat, *Contes de Féés* (1698), Charles Perrault, *Histoires ou Contes du temps passé* (1697), and Jean de Prechac, *Contes moins contes que les autres* (1698)—one can ascertain remarkable differences in their social attitudes, especially in terms of gender and class differences. However, all the fairy tales have one thing in common that literary historians have failed to take into account: they were *not* told or written for children. Even the tales of Perrault. In other words, it is absurd to date the origin of the literary fairy tale for children with the publication of Perrault's tales. Certainly, his tales were popularized and used with children later in the eighteenth century, but it was not because of his tales themselves as individual works of art. Rather, it was because of certain changes in the institution of the literary fairy tale itself.

Up through 1700, there was no literary fairy tale for children. On the contrary, children like their parents *heard* oral tales from their governesses, servants, and peers. The institutionalizing of the literary fairy tale, begun in the salons during the seventeenth century, was for adults and arose out of a need by aristocratic women to elaborate and conceive other alternatives in society than those prescribed for them by men. The fairy tale was used in refined discourse as a means through which women imagined their lives might be improved. As this discourse became regularized and accepted among women and slowly by men, it served as the basis for a

From *Les Contes des fées offerts à Bébè*, c. 1900.

literary mode that was received largely by members of the
aristocracy and haute bourgeoisie. This reception was collective and social, and gradually the tales were changed to introduce morals to children that emphasized the enforcement of
a patriarchal code of *civilité* to the detriment of women, even
though women were originally the major writers of the tales.
This code was also intended to be learned first and foremost
by children of the upper classes, for the literary fairy tale's
function excluded the majority of children who could not
read and were dependent on oral transmission of tales.

Most scholars generally agree that the *literary* development of the children's fairy tale *Beauty and the Beast*, conceived by Madame Le Prince de Beaumont in 1756 as part of
Le Magasin des Enfants, translated into English in 1761 as
*The Young Misses Magazine Containing Dialogues between
a Governess and Several Young Ladies of Quality, Her Schol-*

ars, owes its origins to the Roman writer Apuleius, who published the tale of *Cupid and Psyche* in *The Golden Ass* in the middle of the second century A.D.[12] It is also clear that, in the system used by most folklorists to distinguish different types of tales, the oral folk tale type 425A, the beast bridegroom, played a major role in the literary development. By the middle of the seventeenth century, the Cupid and Psyche tradition was revived in France with a separate publication of Apuleius's tale in 1648 and led La Fontaine to write his long story *Amours de Psyche et de Cupidon* (1669) and Corneille and Molière to produce their tragédie-ballet *Psyché* (1671). The focus in La Fontaine's narrative and the play by Moliére and Corneille is on the mistaken curiosity of Psyche. Her desire to know who her lover is almost destroys Cupid, and she must pay for her "crime" before she is reunited with Cupid. These two versions do not alter the main plot of Apuleius's tale and project an image of women who are either too curious (Psyche) or vengeful (Venus), and their lives must ultimately be ordered by Jove.

All this was changed by Madame D'Aulnoy, who was evidently familiar with different types of beast/bridegroom folk tales and was literally obsessed by the theme of Psyche and Cupid and reworked it or mentioned it in several fairy tales: *Le Mouton* (*The Ram*, 1697), *La Grenouille bienfaisante* (*The Beneficent Frog*, 1698), and *Serpentin Vert* (*The Green Serpent*, 1697), *Gracieuse et Percinet* (*Gracieuse and Percinet*, 1697), *Le Prince Lutin* (*Prince Lutin*, 1697), *La Princesse Félicité et le Prince Adolphe* (*Princess Felicity and Prince Adolph*, 1690). The two most important versions are *The Ram* and *The Green Serpent*, and it is worthwhile examining some of the basic changes in the motifs and plot that break radically from the male tradition of Psyche and Cupid. I must first emphasize that it was Madame D'Aulnoy who prepared the way for the literary version of *Beauty and the Beast*, not Perrault. Though her versions were contrived and simplistic, it was she who initiated changes in the literary fairy tale as institution that have had a far-reaching effect. Madame D'Aulnoy wanted to make the fairy tale part of the living practice of the aristocratic salon, and her tales were elaborated in the parlor games that she and her contemporaries (mainly females) played before they were composed. In the conscious composition of the tales she clearly intended to present a woman's viewpoint with regard to such topics as tender love, fidelity, courtship, honor, and arranged marriages. As a representative artwork, the fairy tale was D'Aulnoy's contribution to a discourse on manners that was to be shared by an intimate group of people, whom she hoped would embrace her ideas. Thus, the fairy tale was not separated from the aristocratic lifestyle of her time but played a representative role indicating her female preferences with regard to the code of civility, preferences that were shared and enunciated in fairy tales by other women.

What were these preferences? Madame D'Aulnoy was by no means a rebel, although she had been in some difficulty at King Louis XIV's court. That is, one must be cautious about labeling her an outspoken critic of patriarchal values or to see feminist leanings in her writings. Nevertheless, as a member of the aristocratic class, who had experienced the benefits of changes in education and social roles for upper-class women, Madame D'Aulnoy created a setting in her tales that placed women in greater control of their destinies than did fairy tales by men, and it is obvious that the narrative strategies of her tales, like those she learned in the salon, were meant to expose decadent practices and behavior among the people of her class, particularly those who degraded independent women.

The Ram and *The Green Serpent* are D'Aulnoy's two most interesting commentaries on what manners a young woman should cultivate in determining her own destiny. The power in all her tales is held by fairies, wise or wicked women, who ultimately judge whether a young woman de-

serves to be rewarded. In other words, if there is a divinity
or transcendental god, it is not the Christian patriarchal
God but a powerful female fairy or a group of fairies. In
The Ram, the heroine is actually punished by a relentless
fairy. Based on the King Lear motif, this tale has Mer-
veilleuse, the youngest daughter of a king, compelled to flee
the court because her father believes mistakenly that she has
insulted him. She eventually encounters a prince who has
been transformed into a ram by a wicked fairy, and she is
gradually charmed by his courteous manners and decides to
wait five years until his enchantment will be over to marry
him. However, she misses her father and two sisters, and
through the ram's kind intervention she is able to visit them
twice. The second time, however, she forgets about returning to the ram, who dies because of her neglect.

In *The Green Serpent*, the heroine Laidronette acts differently. She runs away from home because she is ashamed of
her ugliness. Upon encountering a prince, who, as usual, has
been transformed into a serpent by a wicked fairy, she is at
first horrified. Gradually, after spending some time in his
kingdom of the pagodes, who are exquisite little people that
attend to her every wish, she becomes enamored of him and
promises not to see him and to marry him in two years when
his bewitchment will end. However, even though she reads
the story of Psyche and Cupid, she breaks her promise and
gazes upon him. This breech of promise enables the wicked
fairy Magotine to punish her, and only after Laidronette per-
forms three near-impossible tasks helped by the Fairy Pro-
tectrice is she able to transform herself into the beautiful
Princess Discrète and the green serpent back into a handsome prince. Their love for each other eventually persuades
the wicked fairy Magotine to mend her ways and reward
them with the kingdom of Pagodaland.

The issue at hand in both fairy tales is fidelity and sincerity, or the qualities that make for tenderness, a topic of
interest to women at that time. Interestingly, in Madame

D'Aulnoy's two tales, the focus of the discourse is on the two princesses, who break their promises and learn that they will cause havoc and destruction if they do not keep their word. On the other hand, the men have been punished because they refused to marry old and ugly fairies and seek a more natural love. In other words, Madame D'Aulnoy sets conditions for both men and women that demand sincerity of feeling and constancy, if they are to achieve true and happy love. Nothing short of obedience to the rule of "fairy" civility will be tolerated in D'Aulnoy's tales. The tenderness of feeling was definitely a goal that women sought more than men during D'Aulnoy's times, and her two tales that discuss the proper behavior of young aristocrats have an ambivalent quality to them that makes for interesting reading. D'Aulnoy projects the necessity for women to decide their own destiny, but it is a destiny that calls for women to obey men and actively submit themselves to a rational code that is not really of their making. Thus, while D'Aulnoy wants the fairy tale to have the social function of serving women's interests, there is a dubious side to the manner in which she represents these interests. Active submission to a male code qualified by tenderness does not lead to autonomy, and in fact, though there is this call for female autonomy thoughout most of her tales, it is the prescribed taming of female desire according to virtues associated with male industriousness and fairness that marks the morals attached to the end of each narrative. Of course, it should not be forgotten that D'Aulnoy makes young men tow the "fairy" line of civility. That is, she is extremely critical of forced marriages and makes all her male heroes obey a code of decorum that demands great respect for the tender feelings of the aristocratic woman.

In short, the aesthetic composition and structure of all of D'Aulnoy's fairy tales depended on their social function as game and discourse. Plot is secondary to the discussion of manners and the enactment of proper behavior that serves a moral, and each one of D'Aulnoy's tales ends with a verse *moralité*. Her tales were generally long (thirty-five to forty-five pages), complicated, filled with references to literary works (correct reading), proper dress and manners, and folklore. Though her own writing was not as elegant and subtle as some of the other fairy-tale writers of her time, she set models that they followed.

Madame Gabrielle de Villeneuve was one of her "followers." She published her highly unique version of "Beauty and the Beast" in *La Jeune Amériquaine et les contes marins* in 1740, and it became the classic model for most of the Beauty and the Beast versions that followed in the eighteenth century. Indeed, it served as the basis for Madame Le Prince de Beaumont's most famous tale in 1756, which, in turn, provided the material for Comtesse de Genlis's dramatic adaptation, *The Beauty and the Monster*, in 1785 and for Jean-François Marmontel's libretto for the opera *Zémire et Azor* by André Modeste Grétry in 1788. Most significant by this time is the fact that de Villeneuve wrote a tale of over two hundred pages (the length depends on which edition one reads) and was addressing a mixed audience of bourgeois and aristocratic adult readers. The social function of the fairy tale had changed: its basis was no longer the salon and the games that had been played there. Rather, the literary fairy tale's major reference point was another literary tale or an oral tale and was intended to amuse and instruct the isolated reader, or perhaps a reader who read aloud in a social situation. Whatever the case may have been, it is clear from the length of de Villeneuve's tale, which is more like a small novel, that it was intended for private reading.

Like Madame D'Aulnoy, Madame de Villeneuve was concerned with the self-realization of a young woman, and like the lesson preached by Madame D'Aulnoy, the message of Madame de Villeneuve for women is ambivalent. While all the rules and codes in her fairy tale are set by women— there are numerous parallel stories that involve a fairy kingdom and the laws of the fairies—Beauty is praised most for her submissiveness, docility, and earnestness. In de Villeneuve's version, she does not break her vow to the Beast. Rather she is steadfast and sees through the machinations of her five sisters in time for her to return to her beloved Beast. Then, after she saves him and he is transformed into a charming prince, she is ready to sacrifice herself again by giving up her claim to him because she is merely bourgeois while he is a true nobleman. Her fairy protector, however, debates the prince's mother, who has arrived on the scene, and argues that Beauty's virtues are worth more than her class ranking. Eventually, though the fairy wins the debate, we learn that Beauty is really a princess, who had been raised by her supposed merchant-father to escape death by enemies to her real father, a king.

The justification of Beauty's right to marry is part of a series of discourses on manners that constitute the major theme of the tale: virtuous behavior is true beauty, and only true beauty will be rewarded, no matter what class you are. Beauty (and other characters as well) are tested throughout the tale to determine whether they can tame their unruly feelings (desire, greed, envy, and so forth) and become civilized. For instance, once Beauty arrives at the Beast's castle, she has a series of dreams about an unknown admirer, who is actually the prince, and about a wise fairy, and in these dreams she carries on conversations about responsibility and correct courtship with regard to natural love and obligations. Beauty *always* chooses to fulfill her obligations rather than follow her heart. Although it does turn out that, by fulfilling her obligations, her heart is rewarded, it is plain to see that her destiny depends on self-denial that, she comes to believe, is a wish-fulfillment.

With de Villeneuve's projection of Beauty, the person as an embodiment of the virtue "self-denial," the ground was prepared for a children's version of the Beauty and the Beast tale, and Madame Le Prince de Beaumont did an excellent job of condensing and altering the tale in 1756 to address a group of young misses, who were supposed to learn how to become ladies. In effect, the code of the tale was to delude them into believing that they would be realizing their goals in life by denying themselves. This theme of self-denial, which had very little to do with the female autonomy aristocratic women had sought in the seventeenth century, is closely connected to the *changing* social function of the fairy tale and its inclusion of tales written explicitly for children. First of all, it should be noted once again that the origins of the fairy tale for children cannot be associated with Perrault but with the change in the institution of the fairy tale created by women. As we have seen, the fairy tale served the social function of representation in aristocratic circles in the latter half of the seventeenth century. During the first part of the eighteenth century, the fairy tale was separated from its representative function and became more an artwork that depicted the possibilities for self-realization and was intended mainly for reading audiences of the aristocracy and bourgeoisie. At the same time, writers began to introduce didactic tales and fairy tales with strong messages for children in primers and collections intended for young audiences of the aristocracy and bourgeoisie.

With regard to the "origins" of the fairy tale for children, it is practically impossible to give an exact date, but it is more than likely that, given the shifts in the institution of the fairty tale itself, the fairy tale for children arose in the 1720s and 1730s through the distribution of chapbooks for a broad audience including children. Madame Le Prince de Beaumont's tale was highly unusual because it was one of the first fairy tales, if not the first, written expressly for children, and we must not forget that it was also first published within a book that has a governess tell different kinds of lessons and tales to a group of girls in her charge. Madame Le Prince de Beaumont herself was a governess in

London during the time she wrote her book, and she based its structure on the way she organized the day that she spent with her wards. As Patricia Clancy has pointed out,

she put into practice and perfected many of Fénelon's recommendations on teaching girls. But Fénelon never realised the connection between moral and intellectual education, and mme de Beaumont was thus more ambitious for their minds than he. The lessons were pleasantly interspersed with a good deal of tea-taking and the atmosphere was friendly, even intimate. Her method of teaching was based on free debate and gentle persuasion, which nevertheless did not always avoid some clash of wills. They usually began with one of her fairy tales from which she extrapolated a moral through elaboration and questions, then proceeded to a practical demonstration of physics, history, or geography, or else a commentary on a passage from the Old Testament.[13]

Clearly, there is a shift in the social function of the literary fairy tale as it began to be scripted for children: it was to instruct in an amusing way and was now received by children of the upper classes in the home where lessons were taught by private tutors or by governesses. Moreover, some of the fairy tales were evidently used in schools or in schooling the children of the upper classes. That boys were to be treated differently than girls is apparent from the structure and contents of Madame de Beaumont's book, or in other words, *Beauty and the Beast* originated as a sex-specific tale intended to inculcate a sense of good manners in little girls.

What is this good sense? The sense to sacrifice one's life for the mistakes of one's father, learn to love an ugly beast-man if he is kind and has manners, keep one's pledge to a beast, no matter what the consequences may be. When confronted by her sisters, who accuse her for not being concerned about her father who is sentenced to death for picking a rose, Beauty responds: "Why should I lament my father's death when he is not going to perish? Since the monster is willing to accept one of his daughters, I intend to offer myself to placate his fury, and I feel very fortunate to be in a position to save my father and prove my affection for him." [14]

Beauty is selfless, and perhaps that is why she has no name. She is nameless. All girls are supposed to become "beauties," i.e., selfless and nameless. There is a false power attributed to Beauty as a virtue. By sacrificing oneself, it is demonstrated, the powers that be, here the fairies, will reward her with a perfect husband. The most important thing is to learn to obey and worship one's father (authority) and to fulfill one's promises even though they are made under duress. Ugliness is associated with bad manners like those of her sisters. The beast is not ugly because his manners are perfect. Beauty and the Beast are suited for one another because they live according to the code of civility. They subscribe to prescriptions that maintain the power of an elite class and patriarchal rule.

Madame Le Prince de Beaumont's classic fairy tale enables us to see key features of how the fairy tale was institutionalized for children. The framing conditions of this institutionalization are: (1) the social function of the fairy tale must be didactic and teach a lesson that corroborates the code of civility as it was being developed at that time; (2) it must be short so that children can remember and memorize it and so that both adults and children can repeat it orally; this was the way that many written tales worked their way back into the oral tradition; (3) it must pass the censorship of adults so that it can be easily circulated; (4) it must address social issues such as obligation, sex roles, class differences, power, and decorum so that it will appeal to adults, especially those who publish and publicize the tales; (5) it must be suitable to be used with children in a schooling situation; and (6) it must reinforce a notion of power within the children of the upper classes and suggest ways for them to maintain power.

Of course, there is a more positive reading of *Beauty and the Beast* and the role it played in the institutionalization of the fairy tale. In her day, Madame Le Prince de Beaumont was a progressive thinker who contributed a great deal to raising the esteem of girls and women in England and France. Patricia Clancy explains that "Mme le Prince de Beaumont would by no means have been considered a radical in her own country, yet what she saw and experienced in England fired her with a reforming zeal for both the status and the education of women in society. With her as with most other feminist reformers, the two went hand in hand, and she never ceased to deplore the fact that men denied women education which would make them virtuous, then reviled them for their moral shortcomings." [15] Her primary goal in writing *Beauty and the Beast* was to celebrate the virtuous behavior of her heroine, who courageously chooses to sacrifice herself for the sake of her father. But Beauty's actions give rise to a certain ambivalence that undermines the intentions of Madame Le Prince de Beaumont: Beauty can be admired for her courage and simultaneously deprecated for submitting to the will of two men, her father and the beast. It would seem that she actually seeks to be dominated and to be praised for her submission as a virtuous and courageous act.

Beauty's ambivalent position can be attributed to Madame Le Prince de Beaumont's own ambivalence as reformer who did not want to alter the structure of the family or society and yet wanted to improve the status of women. Therefore, Madame Le Prince de Beaumont rationalized her own compromising role and the submission of women as female desire in her fairy tale. This rationalization of desire is what makes *Beauty and the Beast* so powerful and explains how her version assumed mythic proportions in the eighteenth century and continues to exercise such a compelling appeal up to the present.

In her book, *The Bonds of Love: Psychoanalysis, Femi-*

nism, and the Problem of Domination, Jessica Benjamin sheds light on the subliminal psycho-social force that constitutes the power of *Beauty and the Beast* in the de Beaumont version as a fairy tale that assumes mythic form and pervades our reading with mythic influence. The purpose of Benjamin's study is to understand how domination is anchored in the hearts of the dominated, and she argues that domination is a two-way process, a system involving the participation of those who submit to power as well as those who exercise it. She begins with a focus on the relationship between mother and infant and how the infant in the pre-oedipal phase begins making distinctions between male and female. The male is associated with independence and the female with dependence. That is, the father figure comes to represent the power of protection from the nurturing/smothering power of the mother, and the desire to be protected from the awesome mother leads to positions of master and slave whereby boys and girls learn to regard themselves differently because of their gender-specific socialization. The result is that boys are identified and identify themselves as subjects and girls as objects, especially in the central psychoanalytic model of development, the Oedipus complex.

Benjamin critiques the Freudian construct of the Oedipus complex because of its idealization of the father as liberator and the devaluation of the mother as a subjective threat to the autonomy of both the girl and the boy. In particular, the boy must repudiate the mother as the source of goodness and reject all her other feminine attributes as well while the father is represented as the figure of protector and savior. "The idealization of the father masks the child's fear of his power. The myth of a good paternal authority that is rational and prevents regression purges the father of all terror and, as we will see, displaces it onto the mother, so that she bears the badness for both of them. The myth of the good father (and the dangerous mother) is not easily dispelled." [16]

The father or male principle of rationalization becomes

privileged in the oedipal phase, and Benjamin explains how the paternal ego ideal and the superego push the boy away from intimacy with the mother, while the girl, who can identify and become intimate with the mother, cannot attain recognition from the father, who rejects her attempts at identification. There is no mutual recognition between daughter and father because of this rejection. "Thus the Oedipus complex does not finally resolve the problem of difference, of recognizing an other. The mother is devalued, her power and desire are transferred to the idealized father, and her nurturance is inaccessible. The same phallus that stands for difference and reality also stands for power over the repudiation of women. By assuming the power to represent her sexuality as well as his, it denies women's independent sexuality. Thus masculinity is defined in opposition to woman, and gender is organized as polarity with one side idealized, the other devalued."[17]

Benjamin's feminist reading of the Freudian construct of the Oedipus complex, based on the myth of Oedipus, enables us to see how object relations in the family and society are arranged around the hegemony of paternal authority. As a result, the actual configuration of the Oedipus complex in western families and societies and the manner in which it informs our behavior are predicated on how patriarchy is maintained. And one way in which paternal rule has been reinforced consistently is through fairy tales. Furthermore, *Beauty and the Beast* has been expecially instrumental in rationalizing male domination, gender polarity, and violation because of its formation in the eighteenth century when the middle classes were restructuring family and society in specific patterns that would be internalized through literary socialization.

If we look once more at Madame Le Prince de Beaumont's version of *Beauty and the Beast* in relation to the Oedipus complex and how girls were socialized to desire domination and boys to dominate, we must begin with the fact that Beauty is already in bonds or bonded by the time that we are introduced to her. She lives in a master/slave relationship with her father and accepts all his decisions without question, for he is the ultimate male authority. She has no other model or option because the mother is conveniently dead, wiped out, effaced. In fact, Beauty has already become a type of *Ersatz*-mother, and because of her *willingness* to be dominated and to serve, she is easily exploited by the father.

It is because of Beauty's desire to please the father that she does not hesitate to sacrifice herself to the Beast. In other words, it is not a great step for Beauty to move to the Beast's castle because she is merely exchanging one master for another. What is difficult is the adjustment to the new surroundings and the face of the new master. Once she learns that she can be comfortable in the new surroundings, she is willing to give up her father. In effect, she is placated and pacified because her "new" life, which is really not so new, will be richer and more comfortable. But her position will not be much different, for she is to be the nurturer, the one who sacrifices her body for the desire of the Beast. It is the Beast who *wants* her. She must learn that his desire is her desire just as she had learned that her father's desire was her desire. We are left then with Beauty as an exemplary figure who predicates all her desires on how she can please men, and all this seems reasonable, for they apparently cannot live without her.

Yet, this conclusion is all illusion, for her identity is determined by them. Her function in life is predetermined. Beauty must learn to tame her own desires to fit a male civilizing code in such a way that she appears to be the agent of her own desires. However, in complying with the Beast's desire, she is complying with her father and the socio-psychological prescriptives that promise rewards for masochistic behavior. The reward is a move up the social ladder: Beauty comes from the mercantile class and will be symbolically

From Charles Lamb,
Beauty and the Beast, 1811.

Illustration by
Eduard Corbould, 1985.

From *Beauty and the Beast*,
c. 1900.

Illustration by Edmund Dulac, 1910.

Illustration by
Margaret Tarrant, 1936.

ennobled by marrying the Beast/prince. But her noble action, self-sacrifice for father and Beast, will only strengthen the bonds of domination that will constrain her for the rest of her life. Moreover, it should be stressed that the Beast is also portrayed in a stereotypical "oedipal" manner that rationalizes his will/desire to dominate. Why must he have a virginal daughter to compensate for the father's trespass? Why must he manipulate her to rescue him? Why does he have to be the provider, the keeper of her castle? Why can't he find a way to nurture himself from within? The fact is— if we can speak about facts—Beast's desires have also been scripted or pre-scripted, for he ostensibly knows no other way to win a woman than through power and emotional blackmail. The Beast must play upon preconditioned sentiments in Beauty to feel fulfilled and to become whole as the transformed prince born to rule.

In most of the standard illustrations of *Beauty and the Beast*, Beauty is depicted as compassionate, kind, and considerate. It is through her great compassion and her self-denial that she assumes heroic proportions. The key image in most of the illustrated versions of Madame Le Prince de Beaumont's tale from the eighteenth century to the present reveal Beauty, full of pity leaning over some enormous furry creature or cuddling a freakish monster. What is interesting in all these illustrations is that they also bring out what boys are socialized to expect from young women: total abandonment, nurturing, mercy, obedience, responsibility. No matter what the male/beast is portrayed to resemble—and the imaginations of artists have drawn great pleasure in conceiving the most outlandish creatures imaginable—the female is supposed to curb her disgust and learn to love the Beast for his dignity and power. Or she is supposed to learn to love her chains and bonds. The illustrations in most books generally underline the thesis that the male is a beast despite his noble sentiments and can change with a submissive and tender wife. Males are not supposed to find the tenderness and compassion within themselves; they obtain such sustenance through emotional blackmail and manipulation.

The sentimental if not melodramatic scene of Beauty holding and seemingly rescuing the Beast at the end of the tale is a picture that has been impressed upon our imagination and scripted in thousands of books since Madame Le Prince de Beaumont printed her story in 1756. It was almost immediately frozen as a myth because it complied so "beautifully" with the prescriptions and desires of the male middle class that was solidifying its power in Europe and North America. Fairy tales do not become mythic unless they are in almost perfect accord with the underlying principles of how the male members of society seek to arrange object relations to satisfy their wants and needs. The fairy tales must seem natural and celebrate submission by the opposite sex or the dominated so that the dominated can feel the beauty of their actions.

This is not to say that the dominant pattern and constellation of the fairy tale, frozen as myth, has not been questioned or subverted. Betsy Hearne has pointed to the numerous endeavors by gifted writers and illustrators to suggest alternatives to the rationalization of female submission in the tale. For instance, Albert Smith wrote a mock verse rendition of *Beauty and the Beast* (1853),[18] in which the tone and style of the poem undermined the traditional message of the tale. Even more subversive was Guy Wetmore Carryl's poem, "How Beauty Contrived to Get Square with the Beast," (1902).[19] Here the gambling father, John Jeremy Platt, loses a large amount of money in a card game and obliges his daughter, the beautiful Guinevere, to marry F. Ferdinand Fife, coarse, excessively fat, and rich, to save her father from disgrace. However, the clever and feisty Guinevere drives Ferdinand bonkers and eventually to his death. Over seventy years later, Angela Carter picked up the notion of the decadent father in *The Tiger's Bride* (1979)[20] and elaborated it in a brilliant and unique manner that depicted the mutual fulfillment of desire by two sensual individuals. In commenting on this tale, Sylvia Bryant has argued that the transformation "centers on the girl, not the beast, thus presenting a challenge to the Oedipal myth,"[21] for Carter rewrote the traditional social/sexual patterns, turning them inside out and against themselves to offer the possibility for mutual understanding and respect for otherness. But Carter's work should not be viewed as an isolated or exceptional achievement.

Indeed, it is not by chance that the mythic Oedipus complex came under heavy attack and careful scrutiny during the 1970s when great changes occurred in the family and socialization processes of western countries. Given the questioning of traditional roles in the family, changes at the work place, and the reshaping of stereotypical social and gender expectations, the ideological status quo of the oedipal myth has been compelled to undergo reformation. Consequently, there were many other rescriptings of the frozen mythic constellation of *Beauty and the Beast* such as Janosch's "The Singing, Springing Liontattikin" (1972),[22] Olga Broumas's "Beauty and the Beast" (1977),[23] Robin McKinley's *Beauty* (1978),[24] Sara Henderson Hay's "Sequel" (1982),[25] Tanith Lee's "Beauty" (1983),[26] Peter Redgrove's "The Rose of Leo Mann" (1989),[27] and Gwen Strauss's "The Beast" (1990).[28] All of these versions are very different from one another, but they share a questioning attitude toward the manner in which the fairy tale has become mythicized to impart stereotyped roles of gender behavior in the service of patriarchal rule.

Of course, it is important to bear in mind that they represent the extreme side of the fairy tale as institution within which a heated debate about sexuality and role models has evolved in the last three hundred years. The voices of the traditional and dominant side of the debate since Madame de Beaumont's 1756 tale have continually reproduced the oedipal mythic features to reinforce the theme of female submission and male domination. One need only look at the key versions that have marked our imaginations and served the domestication of desire to verify this tendency. Significant here are Charles Lamb's poem *Beauty and the Beast: or a Rough Outside with a Gentle Heart* (1811),[29] Walter Crane's picture book *Beauty and the Beast* (1875),[30] Andrew Lang's story of "Beauty and the Beast" in *Blue Fairy Book* (1889),[31] and Sir Arthur Quiller-Couch and Edmund Dulac's depiction of "Beauty and the Beast" in *The Sleeping Beauty and Other Tales from the Old French* (1910).[32] All of these renditions have been reproduced countless times up to the present along with thousands of duplications of Madame Le Prince de Beaumont's version as the classical tale, as a means to show how we should script our libidinal urges. Of course, Jean Cocteau also made a major contribution to this classical tradition with his film *La Belle et la Bête* in 1946. Though praised for its innovative artistic experimentation, the major accomplishment of Cocteau's film is in its retelling of the oedipal myth in a more stark and impressionistic manner than had ever been done in print. As Rebecca Pauley has perceptively remarked,

the attraction for Cocteau of the Beaumont *Beauty and the Beast* as an oedipal myth must have been considerable. Numerous elements of the story mark it as a covert tale of incest. First of all, there is no mother present in Beauty's family. She refuses proposals of marriage, stating that she prefers to stay with her father. The request of the rose, symbol of love, perfection, and feminine sexuality, among others, traps her father in a fatal gesture in the realm of the Beast. In the original fable, the father accompanies Beauty to the Beast's castle and spends the night in the same bed with her before returning home. In a later sequence, Beauty returns home to her ailing father and they spend a quarter of an hour in transports of rapture in bed in each other's arms. Even discounting the eighteenth-century tradition of receiving people socially in the bedroom and ruling out any possible libertine overtones, the implication of these two scenes as workings of a thematic incest is undeniable. Moreover, the pairing of the father and daughter reverses the oedipal attraction of the son to the mother, thus offering an incestual mirror of Cocteau's own situation.[33]

However, in view of the development of *Beauty and the Beast* as myth, Cocteau's own situation is incidental. That is, given the manner in which the tale was forged with the oedipal myth as its basic underpinning, Cocteau had no choice but to work through the oedipal motifs by deepening their meaning or posing alternatives to the complex of submission and domination. In this regard, the film has a frightening sadistic side to it, for Cocteau plays a cruel joke on Beauty at the end of the film. Not only does he depict her as totally beholden to her father, but he also has the Beast turn into a prince that resembles Avenant, the very man she did not want to marry.[34]

Cocteau's merit as filmmaker was, in my estimation, to bring out the dark side of the fairy tale while rationalizing the domination of Beauty with an ethereal happy ending. Unfortunately, his film set a model for many others like Roger Vadim's *Beauty and the Beast* (1983), a slavish imitation of Cocteau's work, produced for Shelley Duvall's Faerie Tale Theatre, and Eugene Marner's ludicrous musical, *Beauty and the Beast*, a 1987 Golan-Globus production. As the genre of the fairy tale has expanded to include the cinema and television, the scripts that have been filmed tend to seek new ways of moderating the mythicization of *Beauty and the Beast*, rather than subverting and exploding the motifs so that there can be an invigorating debate and depiction of the problems of domination and submission.

Two recent endeavors to adapt *Beauty and the Beast* for film are indicative of changes in the institutionalization of the fairy tale and transformations of the scripts to accommodate social and family rearrangements so that radical questioning of the oedipal construct can be deflected. In 1987,

Ron Koslow produced the TV series *Beauty and the Beast* for CBS that quickly captured the minds and imaginations of viewers. Set in New York City, this hour-long contemporary dramatization, telecast weekly for two years, began with a wealthy Manhattan woman named Catherine who is raped by thugs and left for dead. Fortunately, a strange monstrous creature from the underworld named Vincent saves her. This noble if not magnificent beast lives with his benevolent "Father" in a maze of subway tunnels with other marginalized people who are more humane than the inhabitants of the upper world of New York. Through Vincent's tender care, Catherine recuperates, and though she returns to this upper world to work as an assistant district attorney, a stronger and more socially conscious woman than she was before the rape, she is totally in love with Vincent, and the episodes of the TV series involve their constant saving and savoring of one another in a platonic relationship that only becomes sensually fulfilled when the series was declared dead in 1990. Though there were positive aspects of this modernization of the traditional *Beauty and the Beast*, such as the independent woman who is not crippled by an oedipal tie to her father and the sensitive, alien male who tries to understand the woman's soul, the plots of each episode were contrived and followed the prescribed criminal-adventure stories depicting the triumph of the noble heroine and hero at the end of each hour. Both Beauty and the Beast remain static after the first episode: they are idealized as mysterious types who are bound to each other in mysterious ways. Yet it is Vincent who represents the better of the two worlds and who sets the higher ideals that cannot be met in the real streets of New York. It is Catherine who must be attracted to this other realm, who must realize how shallow her life is and who acts to meet the expectations that she sees in Vincent's gaze. Consequently, despite the "feminist" touch-up of Beauty in this TV series, the basic plot of submission/domination is merely re-formed to make the con-

temporary beautiful working woman less aware of her
bonds.

This is also the case in the Disney animated film *Beauty
and the Beast* (1992). From the beginning, it would appear
that the Disney studios completely rewrote the traditional
script of de Beaumont's tale and produced a feminist version that would make the old sexist Walt Disney turn over
in his grave. However, despite some clever changes in the
depiction of Beauty, who is a cultivated book lover and a
woman not afraid to speak her mind, we have the exact
same plot of the young woman who sacrifices herself for
her father and for the improvement of a monster such as the
Beast, as well as formulaic musical numbers with cutesy inanimate objects providing comic relief through songs and
jokes. In addition, there is the macho Gaston, who represents the evil violent male side as counterpart to the Beast,
and the bumbling villagers. To a certain extent, as Beauty
makes clear in her first song, she wants to escape the provincialism of the village and wants someone to come along
and rescue her. Now, this same kind of song was also sung
fifty-five years ago in the opening scene of Disney's *Snow
White* (1937), and the same kind of prince rescues Beauty
as the prince who rescued Snow White. So, if there is any
difference in this depiction of Beauty from other fairy-tale
heroines, it is really not in the plot of her life, for it is predetermined: she wants a male to free her, to take her away so
she can submit to his desires, which she believes to be hers.
The only change in the Disney version is that Beauty is a
true elitist, a snob, who doesn't want to mingle with the
coarse villagers.

My critique of the Koslow TV series and the Disney animated film is not intended to dismiss these contemporary
versions of *Beauty and the Beast*, which are entertaining
and artfully produced, but to point to the manner in which
old myths appear in new guises and to situate the repetition
of the traditional story in a cultural historical context that

generates debate just as much as it fosters homogeneity. Today, *Beauty and the Beast* are packaged as attractive commodities that reflect how the fairy tale as institution has immensely changed. The Koslow TV production of *Beauty and the Beast* has been made into a series of novels and comic books and accompanied by commercial video-tapes, T-shirts, insignias, and other artefacts stamped with the familiar faces of Vincent and Catherine. The Disney film *Beauty and the Beast* has also engendered spinoffs of illustrated books with different formats, videotapes, cups, posters, and other articles. In short, *Beauty and the Beast*, as most other fairy tales intended to maintain the mythic-ideological notions of patriarchal rule, is a commodity object produced for a global audience of adults and children that seeks a common denominator to trigger the desire to purchase and become part of the story of *Beauty and the Beast*.

However, whereas the original oral folk tales may have been tales that were indeed part of the shared experience of the listeners, the commodified literary fairy tales and their filmic versions want to induce us to, if not seduce us into, thinking according to the traditional scripts of submission and domination, scripts that may appear to be our stories but have more to do with our taming and domestication than anything else. "Now we have machines to do our dreaming for us," Angela Carter has noted. "But within that video gadgetry might lie the source of a continuation, even a transformation, of storytelling and story-performance. The human imagination is infinitely resilient, surviving colonization, transportation, involuntary servitude, imprisonment, bans on language, the oppression of women."[35] It was in the spirit of such change and resilience that Carter herself wrote radical versions of *Beauty and the Beast* and participated in the filming of *The Company of Wolves*, a subversive revision of *Little Red Riding Hood*, proving that there is a lie to the mythization and homogenization of fairy tales. In the meantime, as the institution of the fairy tale changes, we must become even more aware of those scripts that tame us and prescribe our desires, for they can only become our tales if we review and rewrite them with a strong sense of our own creative powers of transformation.

2. RUMPELSTILTSKIN AND THE DECLINE OF FEMALE PRODUCTIVITY

Rumpelstiltskin is a disturbing fairy tale, not because we never really know the identity of the tiny mysterious creature who spins so miraculously, even when he is named by the queen, the former miller's daughter. It is disturbing because the focus of folklorists, psychoanalysts, and literary critics has centered on Rumpelstiltskin's name and *his* role in the tale despite the fact that the name is meaningless.[1] Indeed, it reveals nothing about Rumpelstiltskin's essence or identity. The naming simply banishes the threatening creature from interfering in the queen's life. Moreover, his role has always been presented in a misleading way. According to the Aarne-Thompson tale type 500, Rumpelstiltskin is categorized as a helper, though he is obviously a blackmailer and oppressor. In short, the categorization has strangely resulted in concern for a villain whose name is just as meaningless as the scholarship that has been absorbed in naming him.

Rumpelstiltskin is a tale about a persecuted woman and female creativity symbolized by spinning. The fact that it has been primarily studied as tale type 500, "The Name of the Helper," for so long by folklorists has more to do with the male bias of scholarship than the specific problem posed by the tale, namely female oppression and the change in the social attitudes toward the metier of spinning and female initiation. To counter these myopic approaches to the tale, I

Illustration by Eugen Napoleon Neureuther, 1882.

shall explore questions of female productivity and relate *Rumpelstiltskin* to other tales about spinners and the sociohistorical development of spinning in the eighteenth and nineteenth centuries.[2]

Before I begin my exploration, I should like to qualify my argument to make it clear that I am not entirely dismissing the motif of naming, but endeavoring to refocus attention on the substantial features of the tale that, in my opinion, constituted its meaning within a historical tradition of female initiation of spinners (mainly in Europe) that has become obfuscated. There is no doubt that the naming of the blackmailer/persecutor/demon fulfills an important *function* in the tale, and this function as essential episode has several purposes:

1. As a riddle, the naming added tension and humor to the narrative and was obviously related to various puzzles and games within the oral tradition of different cultures. The naming is comic relief and points to the optimistic disposition of the tale, intended to demonstrate how the spinner can overcome obstacles and realize her desires and purpose in life.

2. The naming demonstrates the cleverness, skill, and luck of the spinner, who liberates herself and comes into her own through guessing the right name.

3. To name someone or something has always been linked to gaining power over the unknown. To name is to know, to recognize, to become secure through knowledge so that one can protect oneself. In this regard, the naming is the appropriate ending for the spinner, who has come to know herself and identify her enemies. Though the name Rumpelstiltskin may have no revelatory meaning, the act of naming itself is significant.

4. The significance of the naming, the act, is in the shifts that the naming undergoes, depending on the version one reads or hears. As we shall see, the act can be a designation of the oppressor, a separation from the devil, a capitulation to male authority, or a completion of the initiation as spinner.

5. The act says something about the *spinner* and not about the tiny figure, who has intervened in her life. By acting, she defines her

fate or allows her fate to be defined for her. The act of naming completes the spinning as a productive and narrative act. As Karen Rowe suggests, "in the history of folktale and fairy tale, women as storytellers have woven or spun their yarns, speaking at one level to a total culture, but at another to a sisterhood of readers who will understand the hidden language" (1986:57).

If the naming is meaningful in the tale, it is only in relation to the initiation that the female spinner undergoes. By depicting the protagonists learning how to spin and to maintain control of spinning as production, the *Rumpelstiltskin* narratives celebrated at one time the self-identification of a young woman. However, these narratives also indicate how men inserted themselves into the initiation process and intervened to appropriate the narrative tradition. Consequently, initiation became framed within a male discourse.

To demonstrate how initiation became manipulation (or how persecution has been overlooked) within the tradition of spinning tales, I want to make clear from the onset that I shall be dealing with the Brothers Grimm 1857 version of *Rumpelstiltskin* and treating it as a *literary fairy tale*, which has antecedents in folklore and in the French literary tradition, namely Mademoiselle L'Héritier's *Ricdin-Ricdon* (1798).[3] After discussing the nature of the changes that the Grimms made in the oral rendition, which they had recorded in the Ölenberg manuscript of 1810, I shall focus on the spinning aspect of the tale that has received so little attention from scholars, even though it is the most consistent motif in almost all the oral and literary versions published up to the present. Indeed, as early as 1898, the famous British folklorist Edward Clodd, who wrote the first important study of tale type 500 called "Tom Tit Tot" in the English tradition, remarked, "Wellnigh all the heroines in the 'Tom Tit Tot' group are set the task of spinning, in a magic space of time, a large quantity of flax, or, as in the Swedish variant, the still harder task of spinning straw into gold, and so forth. Prominence is therefore given to the wheel and distaff as woman's typical occupation."[4]

It is time now that scholarship give back prominence to the wheel and distaff in the "Rumpelstiltskin" tradition.

In the Ölenberg manuscript of 1810, the "Rumpenstünzchen" version of *Rumpelstiltskin* is based on an anonymous oral tale that Jacob Grimm recorded in 1808 in Hessia. It reads as follows:

Rumpenstünzchen

Once upon a time there was a little maiden who was given a bunch of flax to spin, but she continually spun only gold thread from it and could not produce yarn. She was very sad and sat down on the roof and began to spin, and for three days she only spun gold. Then a tiny man appeared and said, "I'll help you out of all your troubles. Your young prince will come by and marry you and take you away, but you must promise me that your first child will be mine."

The little maiden promised him everything. Soon thereafter a handsome young prince came by, and he took her with him and made her his bride. After one year, she bore him a handsome boy. Then the tiny man appeared at her bedside and demanded the baby. She offered him everything else instead, but he accepted nothing. He gave her three days' time, and if she did not know his name on the last, she would have to give him the child. The princess thought about it for a long time. She thought for two days but still did not come up with the name. On the third, she ordered one of her faithful maids to go into the forest from which the tiny man had come. That night the maid went out and saw the little man riding on a cooking ladle around a large fire and crying out: "If the princess only knew that my name was Rumpenstünzchen."

The maid rushed with this news to the princess, who was very happy to hear it. At midnight the tiny man came and said, "If you don't know my name, I'm going to take the child with me."

Then she guessed all sorts of names until she finally said, "Could it possibly be that your name is Rumpenstünzchen?"

When the tiny man heard this, he became horrified and said,

Illustration by Charles Folkard, 1911.

"The devil must have told you," and he flew out of the window on the cooking ladle.[5]

By the time the brothers revised the text for the publication of the first volume of their *Kinder- und Hausmärchen* in 1812, they had made various changes based on a tale told to them by Dortchen Wild and material from Johann Fischart's *Gargantua* (1582). Later they combined this tale with another oral version told to them by Lisette Wild, and there are also clear signs that they were aware of the French literary version *Ricdin-Ricdon* by Mademoiselle L'Héritier,[6] whose tale also influenced the Grimms' *The Three Spinners*. In short, the 1857 *Rumpelstiltskin* is an amalgamation of literary and oral tales that the Grimms carefully reworked to represent the dilemma of a young peasant woman who cannot spin to save herself. Moreover, as Gonthier-Louis Fink has maintained,[7] the oral tradition had undergone a crucial change during the Enlightenment with the result that the duping of a prince was combined with the mocking of the devil in a tale of wish-fulfillment on the part of the lower classes. What he, however, forgets to note is that the storytellers were probably female spinners and that the oral tale of the seventeenth and eighteenth centuries underwent a literary transformation at the same time that the metier of spinning was undergoing a significant transformation because of industrialization throughout Great Britain and the European continent.

Clearly, by the time the Grimms had begun hearing the oral tales and reading the literary versions, the nature of spinning, the control of spinning as a craft, and the attitude toward spinning became crystallized in their final version of *Rumpelstiltskin*. If we compare *Rumpenstünzchen* (1810) with *Rumpelstiltskin* (1857), we shall see that (whether consciously or unconsciously) the Grimms were making a social-historical statement about the exploitation of women as spinners and the appropriation of the art/craft of spinning by men. First, let us examine the crucial changes, which the Grimms made after recording the oral version.

Rumpenstünzchen	*Rumpelstiltskin*
1. There is simply a little maiden (without a father) who spins flax into gold.	A poor miller boasts that his daughter can spin straw into gold.
2. The maiden's predicament is her failure to do her job properly.	The predicament of the miller's daughter is the lie told by her father that makes it seem she can perform an extraordinary feat.
3. The maiden willingly agrees to the conditions set by the small man.	The miller's daughter is threatened by the king. She later accepts the little man's bargain under duress.
4. The maiden, now a princess, sends out a female servant to solve the riddle of Rumpenstünzchen's name.	The miller's daughter, now a queen, sends out a male messenger to solve the riddle of Rumpelstiltskin's name.
5. Rumpenstünzchen flies away on a cooking ladle.	Rumpelstiltskin tears himself in two.

Crucial in both versions is the *predicament* of a peasant girl who cannot perform adequately. That is, the plot of the tale depends on the nature of the spinning, on the inability of the girl to do her job as a spinner according to social expectations. Without this predicament there is no tale. No need to tell the tale. And as we all know, tales are born out of necessity and desire.

We do not know who the source of the *Rumpenstünzchen* version was, but it is interesting to note that the tale would appear to represent a peasant woman's perspective. First of all, it was more important to be able to spin flax into yarn than into gold for a spinner. In fact, yarn was her gold. Her value was measured by her industriousness and yarn, and gold would have been a preposterously ironical symbol of her clumsiness and inability to learn to spin correctly, i.e., the gold that most people would cherish is *not* valuable in women's eyes because spinning is tied to regeneration, narration, and creation. So the entire tale is a spoof. This is not to say that a peasant woman would not want to turn flax into gold and wanted gold, but every peasant woman knew that she stood a better and realistic chance of finding a man and earning a livelihood by spinning flax into yarn. Therefore, the little man as proper spinner is important and knows his worth as does she. He does not need to blackmail her. He is more a prophet or miracle-maker, who makes a straightforward bargain, and when he returns to receive the firstborn child, he offers another deal in the form of a riddle to see if she has perhaps become smarter than she was before. She passes this test by sending out a *female* servant, who discovers Rumpenstünzchen's name, and the little man is not killed but accuses the devil of betraying him. Symbolically he flies through the window on a cooking ladle. That is, he is banished by a utensil associated with women, who have united to defeat him.

In a reading of this tale that makes spinning the central theme, we can see that the narrative concerns a young woman who advances in society through spinning. The little man could be interpreted as a master spinner, who wants to receive his payment after teaching her the value of spinning. Symbolically he is the miraculous agent who sets things right for her by doing what must be properly done, namely spinning flax into yarn. By the time he demands payment, she is capable of rectifying her mistake. The bargain was an unfair one. She was exploited at a time when she was naive and clumsy. With the help of another woman, she names her exploiter, who is carried away on a female utensil.

The Grimms altered the *Rumpenstünzchen* version in a manner that undermines the value of spinning and the autonomy of the spinner. In their literary narrative, it is apparent that they were concerned to provide clearer motivation, better transition, and a fluid, logical plot. Here the miller's daughter is totally at the mercy of men. In fact, her whole life is framed by men: her father the boaster, a king the oppressor, Rumpelstiltskin the blackmailer, and a messenger the savior. The only thing she appears capable of doing is giving birth to a baby. Even spinning is not taken seriously, for it is esteemed only if she can spin straw into gold. This is not a valid test of a young woman within an initiation process determined by other spinners because the Grimms did not really grasp the value of spinning for women. For the Grimms, the good woman was the woman who knew her place, and the tale concerns a woman who is put in her place and given her place by men. It is a tale of domestication in which the art of spinning flax into yarn becomes irrelevant. Clearly, the Grimms' literary version of *Rumpelstiltskin* makes the male presence in the tale crucial for determining the predicament and fate of the miller's daughter, whereas the maiden decided her own fate in conflict with men in *Rumpenstünzchen*. As a result, it is possible to argue that the two tales represent a female and male perspective about women and spinning at the beginning of the nineteenth century.

However, there is a similarity between the two versions that should be taken into account before we consider the connection of the tales to the metier of spinning in Europe. Unlike the Grimms' tale, *The Three Spinners*, these two versions place spinning in the hands of *men*. Whether it is spinning flax into yarn or straw into gold, the *art* of spinning has been appropriated by men, and it does not matter what they are called. They are, bluntly speaking, the men who control the means of production, and women are beholden to them. In fact, I would argue that control over spinning and the value of spinning are the key themes of the *Rumpelstiltskin* type tales, which have been erroneously categorized under the label "The Name of the Helper."

In her provocative study about women and spinning, *Wie den Frauen der Faden aus der Hand genommen wurde: Die*

Spindel der Notwendigkeit, Gerburg Treusch-Dieter has maintained, "It is a historical fact that the spindle remained in the hands of women until the invention of the spinning machine. Spinning can be considered as the *paradigm* of female productivity."[8] Treusch-Dieter studies the evolution of spinning as a craft and analyzes artifacts, symbols, and documents from a period several centuries before the birth of Christ to the nineteenth century to demonstrate how spinning as an art form was an invention of women and a manifestation of female productivity.[9] When a woman spun, she not only had the thread in her hand but also the wool or flax out of which it originated. In other words, she held the distaff in the left and spun the yarn with the right. In Greek mythology, the spindle was an image of the cosmos that contained the Platonic spindle of necessity in it. The fates of the souls about to be reborn are brought about by the spindle and prepared by it. As a parthogenetic machine, the spindle does not give the soul its existence, but it prepares the soul for being. It resides in a middle realm before birth and after death. Without the spindle as the embodiment of female productivity, there is no existence; it/she creates the basic conditions for all being. As Treusch-Dieter points out, if we examine the way the spindle of necessity functions, we can see how it has served to determine basic aspects of female productivity:

> Continual rotation, mere doing. Whatever is produced disappears before it assumes existence. At the same time it originates as something new again.
> The level of an objectivization in time is not reached. The activity of the spindle does not have a historical relevance. It is the continual now without a present. Air.
> The activity of the spindle is a pure natural phenomenon. Without the assistance of the person occupied in it, on it, and on top of it, it moves itself by itself, brings itself out of itself. Seemingly.[10]

Treusch-Dieter argues that, as the primary symbol of female productivity, the spindle was mythicized and mystified because it was that which was not supposed to be true. In other words, female productivity was not to be recognized. Therefore, it appeared only in an unreal form. "A circle made out of fire and water surrounds Plato's spindle. Lethe, the water of forgetting. It is that which is forbidden to be looked upon and known. Since its place is nowhere, it is just as if it is excluded from reality." [11]

The spindle as myth and mysterious, the mysterious myth, was transformed into such a symbol, according to Treusch-Dieter, because society, if not civilization, was very much dependent on spinning as female productivity. Spinning was not only the basic mode of production in the house, court, and temple but it also provided one of the first products for the ancient markets of commodity exchange.

That meant for women, that the demand for a surplus product was placed on them in the earliest phase in the development of civilization. That which is made out of yarn and thread is easy and long-lasting. It is as if it were created just for commodity exchange. Since the production of the raw material for spinning was a human matter and occupation, there were no limits set on it, whether it was in the form of raising sheep or planting flax. The result was that this raw material, *the* tow (wool or flax) became the embodiment of the natural wealth, the absolute symbol of the "material of life." And it became the inexhaustible source of work for women. [12]

From the early formation of grazing societies up to the nineteenth century, women participated in almost all the work that concerned spinning. They took care of the animals and helped plant the flax; they cleaned and prepared the wool and roasted, broke, and hackled the flax. They did practically all the spinning. That is, spinning became the privilege of women, and it was considered their domain also because it allowed for their domestication. [13]

This domestication was important in a positive sense because it enabled men to profit from the surplus production of women that led to primitive accumulation and also enabled men to deny their dependence on women's productivity by moving it out of their sight, inside, in the home. On the other hand, this domestication enabled women to separate themselves from men, to draw a line, and to maintain power over their own productivity, viewed as a parthogenetic symbol. The spindle was associated with the womb, her ultimate power of creativity, her autonomy. The woman as spinner was the provider of the thread of life, the producer of clothes that was one the earliest marks of civilization distinguishing humans from animals, and the producer of surplus profit.

Spinning as productivity also furnished the basis for all sorts of cultural activities. By the late European Middle Ages, spinning was common in all the households of each social strata, the peasantry, the bourgeoisie, and the aristocracy.[14] The production of thread, yarn, and cloth for garments was considered so important that, by the seventeenth century, numerous courts had begun primitive factory systems by housing spinners at the court to maintain the production of clothes. Spinning rooms could be found in peasant houses and also middle-class houses, and they were both a work and social place for women, children, and men. Often groups of young women were supervised in a separate dwelling, a *Spinnstube*, where they could work undisturbed and exchange stories and pleasantries. This is especially true for the peasantry, which was the largest class to maintain spinning as female productivity up through the nineteenth century. As Hans Medick has documented about the villages of Southwest Germany,

separate Spinnstuben for the youth of both sexes alongside forms of familial and neighborhood Spinnstuben were allowed. The overwhelmingly largest part of the village participants was composed of unmarried youth of the female sex. In places of intensive rural textile production, the corresponding form of male gatherings existed, but were never so important in terms of numbers . . .

The appearance of the male village youth at the Spinnstube of the women, at least for a short time during the evening (usually between 9 and 10 at night) was a usual practice. Here the rules of the "game of the sexes" were determined very strongly by the women present, and not, as if often supposed, exclusively or even to a large extent by the men of the village.[15]

In a good part of Europe, where spinning was prevalent, peasant women would work in spinning rooms or a room that housed the spindle from morning until evening, and the men and young boys would join them in the evening, where there might be some singing, games, dancing, eating, and storytelling. It was the place where young men could find their match, and women could demonstrate their skills to win a husband. In fact, in some instances the young men were prohibited from frequenting the spinning rooms at certain times because they distracted the younger women.[16] Obviously, conditions varied from region to region in Europe, but there is a great deal of evidence to demonstrate that the spinning rooms were types of "cultural or social centers"[17] up to the beginning of the nineteenth century and that tales were exchanged by women as well as men to pass the time of day.

What were these tales? To be more precise, what were the kinds of tales that concerned spinners and spinning? Marianne Rumpf has distinguished several different types, which are all related. Since industriousness in preparing the flax and wool for spinning, along with spinning itself, was considered a key quality of peasant women, especially young women of marriage age, numerous stories focused on how a young woman proved her mettle through diligent spinning to gain a husband or rise in society. The major theme involved the initiation of a young woman as spinner and wish-fulfillment: a good marriage earned through spinning and hard work. This theme was varied in different ways. Some tales were humorous anecdotes (*Schwänke*) that poked fun at young women who were clumsy at spinning or did not know how to spin and needed the help of older women or a miracle to show they were good spinners. Indeed, if a young woman was not a good spinner, her parents would be ashamed of her and would lie to their neighbors, pretending their daughter was the best of all spinners. Such lying served as the basis for the plot of numerous other tales, and the young woman, trapped by a preposterous boast, had to find miraculous help to prove that she was as good a spinner as was claimed.

Often tales about spinners combined motifs from other stories such as the duping of the devil or a member of the upper class. Here again wish-fulfillment played a role: the young woman overcomes adversity, outsmarts the devil, and passes herself off as a miraculous spinner so that she can rise in society and marry a king or prince. Another element added to spinning stories concerns guessing games, puzzles, and riddles. These activities helped pass the time in spinning rooms, and numerous tales made use of guessing and solving riddles to build suspense in a tale. More than anything, however, the riddle was generally a narrative device and was not intended to become the central focus of the tale. As Marianne Rumpf states: "There is plenty of evidence in those tales with a spinning-helper that they were originally riddle tales which must have also emanated from a spinning milieu. What is striking is that in all the variants the name to be guessed is different each time. They are never the usual names of people rather a teasing name, pet name, or nickname like *Zistel im Körbel, Purzinigele, Kugerl, Waldkügele, Hahnenkickerle, Winterkölbl, Springhunderl, Kruzimugeli, Ziligackerl, Friemel Frumpenstiel, Hoppentinchen* and many others." [18]

In other words, the name is irrelevant, and the guessing game is mainly important because it provides suspense in the narrative structure of the tale. The major theme from beginning to end, however, is *spinning* as a creative and productive act, important for the woman to control, for spinning will decide her fate. Even in those humorous tales in which the young woman dreams of never having to spin anymore, she

Illustration by Ernst Liebermann, 1929.

knows that it is through spinning that she must prove her
worth. For a woman, to spin is to create, to produce the
threads that will hold society together. It is through spinning
that a young woman was initiated into society. In fact the
spindle and spinning formed the focal point of the European
peasant family during Middle Ages up to the nineteenth century, when this mode of female productivity was ultimately
eroded and denigrated.

Actually, this process of erosion began earlier. With the
invention of the spinning machine in 1764 by James Har-
greaves, spinning was gradually taken out of the hands of
women and taken over by men. As Treusch-Dieter remarks,

it is certain that the spinning machine replaced the spinner. In view
of the fundamental meaning of female productivity in the form
represented by the spinner, one can conclude that the thousand-
year-long, *unmediated* independence of the woman as womb and

spindle, understood as a barrier protecting her production, collapsed forever. Along with this collapse, the last barrier protecting the exploitation of the cosmos fell so that it was now raw material, totally without taboos, at the disposal of anyone. Machinery took the place of the directly generating and engendering woman, and from now on it took care of providing the basics of society. The paradigmatic meaning of the "Jenny" (the name of the first spinning machine), from whose parthenogenetic womb the great industry emanated, even if it was driven by steam, allows one to make such a generalization.[19]

Major changes occurred during the latter part of the eighteenth century and throughout the nineteenth century. In a highly significant essay entitled "Rumpelstiltskin's Bargain," Jane Schneider has pointed out that spinning and the manufacture of linen had been encouraged by mercantilists and manufacturers from the seventeenth to the nineteenth century to establish indigenous markets and increase the population. To the extent that they were successful, their success was owing to their promises of improving the marriage chances of young women, providing employment for women and men, and creating markets for surplus production. However, this intensification of linen production began to decrease by the end of the eighteenth century because cotton became cheaper to manufacture through new technology. In addition, flax did harm to the soil, and the process of preparing flax for spinning was long and arduous. Therefore, the promotion of flax and spinning became a dubious affair, and peasants were divided among themselves as to whether flax production was profitable for their families. For the most part, the merchant capitalist intensification led to their losing control of their own work and markets, and according to Schneider, the promoters of flax interfered with their traditional work and rituals and were regarded by some as "demonic" and alien just as Rumpelstiltskin was associated with sinister, outside forces. As Schneider states, "It seems to me that the fairies and trolls,

dwarfs and green men, of the linen districts became demonic to the degree linen production intruded on their living
space, over and above the prior intrusion of subsistence
crops and livestock. For, while promising love and money,
the linen promotion schemes undermined not only an earlier autonomy and earlier social ties, but also earlier uses
and users of the land."[20]

What was most disastrous for women was the fact that
the actual spinning of yarn and thread became more and
more mechanized. Instead of women, men attended and
took care of the spinning machines. These machines were
taken out of the house, and small factories were established.
Although women continued to work in these factories, they
gradually gave way to men, and in those cases where wom-
en remained on the job, the management was predomi-
nantly in the hands of men. The surplus products and profits that women supplied were taken over by the owners of
the machines and factories. To be sure, spinning continued
throughout the nineteenth century, but the role of the woman as spinner had become more or less degraded. In fact,
Patricia Baines demonstrates in *Spinning Wheels, Spinners
and Spinning*, spinning as a craft was practically destroyed
during the nineteenth century, and this destruction strongly
affected women of the peasantry and working classes. It is
not by chance that there is a change in the Western social
attitude toward spinning by women and that it is marked by
a shift in the meaning of the word *Spinster*. *The Oxford
Universal Dictionary* states that *spinster* was "appended to
names of women, orig. to denote their occupation, but sub-
sequently as the proper legal designation of one unmarried"[21] in Middle English. By 1719, a spinster was synonymous with old maid. In French the term for spinster is
vielle fille. There is a connection to *filer* or *filare*: to spin. In
German, *eine alte Spinne* is an ugly old woman. To spin is
spinnen, and *spinnen* can also mean to babble in a crazy way.

These changes in social attitudes toward spinning and the

actual changes in spinning production are important to grasp
if we are also to comprehend the central theme of *Rumpelstiltskin* and the other spinning tales in the Grimms' *Kinder-
und Hausmärchen*. The very first literary form of *Rumpelstiltskin*, Mademoiselle L'Héritier's *Ricdin-Ricdon*,[22] demonstrates that spinning was cherished by the aristocracy at
the end of the seventeenth and beginning of the eighteenth
century. The queen is most eager to employ Rosanie as a spinner and cherishes all the articles that Rosanie magically produces. We know that numerous French courts had constructed spinning rooms for women to produce much-needed
cloth, and there was a great demand for gifted spinners at the
time that Mademoiselle L'Héritier wrote her tale. Interestingly, her model spinner, Rosanie, takes possession of the
devil's magic wand (i.e., phallus) to create an image that satis-
fies if not exceeds society's expectations. She does *not* spin
straw into gold but rather flax into yarn and thread. Nor does
she marry a prince on false pretenses. She exposes herself and
attains her place at court because of her "natural" virtues. Of
course, it does turn out that she was of noble birth, but this
discovery only reinforces the notion that there is a "natural"
hierarchy and proper manner of behavior that is best exem-
plified by the aristocracy.

In the case of Rosanie, spinning brings out her qualities
of diligence, loyalty, and especially honesty, for she admits
that her spinning is dependent on the miraculous intervention of supernatural powers. She spins her story, and her
fate is entwined with her aristocratic origins and courageous efforts to improvise and to overcome deceit according
to the norms of the French civilizing process and the values
established by French aristocratic women, who wanted to
proclaim their precocity. Throughout the entire tale, spinning and female creativity remain the central concern and
are upheld as societal values that need support, especially
male support.

This theme was reproduced and changed in oral and other

literary versions of this tale during the eighteenth century. In fact, there is a fascinating fairy tale entitled *Der kurze Mantel* (1789-92), translated as *The Cloak*,[23] which focuses entirely on the positive aspects of the spinning tradition in Germany. It was written by Bendedikte Naubert, one of the most popular authors of this period, and portrays Frau Holle or Mother Hulla as a type of patron saint of spinners. In Naubert's version, spinning remains in the hands of women, for Fraue Holle guides the two female protagonists, the young Genelas and the wise woman Rose, to appreciate the art of spinning that enables them each to marry as they desire. In fact, it is through spinning a magnificent cloak that the two women realize their potential and are able to move away from a corrupt court to a more utopian setting by the end of the narrative.

The Grimms knew this tale, but by the time that they began recording their spinning tales, there was a more *ambivalent* attitude toward spinning. Given the long period (1808-1857) during which time *Rumpelstiltskin* and their other spinning tales were collected, published, and revised, they provide an unusual composite picture of spinning and attitudes toward women and spinning during a key transitional period in the production of thread and yarn.

If we return to *Rumpelstiltskin* now, we can see more clearly that the tale is not only about the persecution of a young woman, but it is also about the merchant capitalist intensification of linen manufacture and the appropriation of her means of production through which she would normally establish her quality and win a man. The miller's daughter cannot spin straw into gold, and there is not even any mention that she can spin. She must depend on a man, who has miraculous powers of spinning (almost like a machine), and her only quality lies within her capacity to reproduce the species. She is reduced to reproduction and placed at the mercy of men. This image of the young spinner's fate does not stem from the misogynous predilections of the Grimms. Rather it is an interesting reflection, as I read it, of the change in the situation of women as spinners in the nineteenth century.

If we consider some of the other spinning tales that the Grimms revised and included in their collection, we can see that they contain divergent views that reflect the high value placed on spinning but also show that changes in social attitudes were under way.[24] For instance, in such tales as *Mother Holle, The Spindle, Shuttle, and Needle,* and *The Hurds,* the emphasis is placed on the industriousness and diligence of the young woman as spinner who wins a prince. This is not the case in *The Lazy Spinner* and *The Three Spinners,* in which women use cunning to avoid spinning. Here spinning is denigrated either as exhausting work or work that can lead to disfiguration. Though it may lead to marriage, spinning is not regarded with much esteem, reflecting the change in social attitudes toward the metier. It is especially interesting to note that *The Three Spinners,* which is clearly based on Mademoiselle L'Héritier's literary tale, *Ricdin-Ricdon,* reverses the initiation process of the young woman. Mademoiselle L'Héritier's tale holds spinning in high regard and as the means through which Rosanie can prove herself and become a valuable member of society. The young woman in *The Three Spinners* never learns how to spin and accepts the help of the three spinners only so that she will never have to spin in her life, indicating how spinning would be regarded in Europe toward the end of the nineteenth century.

Once again, Schneider makes an important point about the ambivalent viewpoint toward spinning as the central theme in *Rumpelstiltskin* and other spinning tales:

Note that the demonized spirits of the spinning tales did not seek to eliminate linen manufacture. On the contrary, Rumpelstiltskin and the witch-like crones contributed to its development, magically producing yarn and facilitating the status mobility through marriage that the linen schemes promised as the reward for diligent spinning. The spirits did, however, claim a piece of the action through their malicious sabotage of human reproduction. As such they splendidly dramatized the core dilemma of the linen "proto-industry." Inextricably mixing opportunity with danger, it rescued poor women from celibacy, shame, or migration only to jeopardize their and their children's social support and health. Caught in this dilemma, the producers crystallized their ambivalence toward the promotion of linen in tales of misfits like Rumpelstiltskin, who were nasty and yet helpful at the same time.[25]

The result of this ambivalence is an ironical shift in the way *Rumpelstiltskin* has been received and interpreted by modern educated readers. In fact, the change in technology and social conventions that brought about mixed social attitudes toward spinning led folklorists and other critics in the twentieth century to neglect the central issue of female productivity and persecution in *Rumpelstiltskin*. After all, spinning rarely takes place in the home, and if it does, the woman generally does it as a hobby. It is *unnecessary* work, just as weaving is generally considered as unnecessary woman's work, often dismissed or elevated as arts and crafts. Whatever the case may be, the issue concerning the neglect of female productivity in *Rumpelstiltskin* has ramifications for the way we analyze and interpret folk and fairy tales.

A few questions come to mind. Why aren't the tale-type categories established by Aarne-Thompson reevaluated and questioned by folklorists?[26] Put another way: wouldn't it be more useful to conceive social-historical categories for explaining why certain types of tales originated? Why is it that most of the psychoanalytic interpretations of *Rumpelstiltskin* are phallocentric? Why does the male in the tale receive most of the attention, when the basic plot concerns female productivity? Clearly, numerous tale types are either gender-specific or occupation-specific and emanate out of changing attitudes toward work and societal norms. Whether oral or literary, tales are often strategies developed by tellers and writers to convey their opinions and wishes with regard to value placed on certain occupations and particular forms of initiation. Refocusing our attention on substantive categories instead of formal attributes enables us to situate tales in their social-historical context and to grasp the dialogic role they play in constituting the civilizing process outlined in Norbert Elias's works.

Coincidentally, Mademoiselle L'Héritier's *Ricdin-Ricdon* made its appearance at the dawn of modern western civilization and represented spinning and female productivity as values that were important to the maintenance of civilization. By the beginning of the nineteenth century, these values were in danger of being extinguished. The thread was taken out of the hands of women, and they were no longer able to spin with fate. *Rumpelstiltskin* marked the end of an important aspect of female productivity and a major shift in the civilizing process for women that brought about greater dependence on men. In this regard, the problems raised by *Rumpelstiltskin* and obfuscated largely by male scholars now provide a significant key for grasping many of the major conflicts in the work place and in academia, and feminists today are appropriately picking up the thread that the miller's daughter was obliged to let fall.

3. BREAKING THE DISNEY SPELL

It was not once upon a time, but in a certain time in history, before anyone knew what was happening, Walt Disney cast a spell on the fairy tale, and it has been held captive ever since. He did not use a magic wand or demonic powers. On the contrary, Disney employed the most up-to-date technological means and used his own "American" grit and ingenuity to appropriate the European fairy tales. His technical skills and ideological proclivities were so consummate that his signature has obfuscated the names of Charles Perrault, the Brothers Grimm, Hans Christian Andersen, and Collodi. If children or adults think of the great classical fairy tales today, be it *Snow White, Sleeping Beauty,* or *Cinderella*, they will think Walt Disney. Their first and perhaps lasting impressions of these tales and others will have emanated from a Disney film, book, or artefact. Though other filmmakers and animators produced remarkable fairy-tale films, Disney managed to gain a cultural stranglehold on the fairy tale, tightened by the recent productions of *Beauty and the Beast* (1991) and *Aladdin* (1992). The man's spell over the fairy tale seems to live on even after his death.

But what does the Disney spell mean? Did Disney achieve a complete monopoly of the fairy tale during his lifetime? Did he imprint a particular *American* vision on the fairy tale through his animated films that dominates our perspective

Illustration by Charles Folkard, 1911.

today? And, if he did manage to cast his mass-mediated spell on the fairy tale so that we see and read the classical tales through his lens, is that so terrible? Was Disney a nefarious wizard of some kind that we should lament his domination of the fairy tale? Wasn't he just more inventive, more skillful, more in touch with the American spirit of the times than his competitors, who also sought to animate the classical fairy tale for the screen?

Of course, it would be a great exaggeration to maintain that Disney's spell totally divested the classical fairy tales of their meaning and invested them with his own. But it would not be an exaggeration to assert that Disney was a radical filmmaker who changed our way of viewing fairy tales, and that his revolutionary technical means capitalized on American innocence and utopianism to reinforce the social and political status quo. His radicalism was of the right and the righteous. The great "magic" of the Disney spell is that he animated the fairy tale only to transfix audiences and divert their potential utopian dreams and hopes through the false promises of the images he cast upon the screen. But before we come to a full understanding of this magical spell, we must try to understand what he did to the fairy tale that was so revolutionary and why he did it.

In order to grasp the major impact of film technology on the fairy tale and to evaluate Disney's role during the pioneer period of fairy-tale animation, it is first necessary to summarize the crucial functions that the literary fairy tale as institution had developed in middle-class society by the end of the nineteenth century:

1. It introduced notions of elitism and separatism through a select canon of tales geared to children who knew how to read.

2. Though it was also told, the fact that the fairy tale was printed and in a book with pictures gave it more legitimacy and enduring value than an oral tale which disappeared soon after it was told.

3. It was often read by a parent in a nursery, school, or bedroom to soothe a child's anxieties, for the fairy tales for children were optimistic and were constructed with the closure of the happy end.

4. Although the plots varied and the themes and characters were altered, the classical fairy tale for children and adults reinforced the patriarchal symbolical order based on rigid notions of sexuality and gender.

5. In printed form the fairy tale was property and could be taken by its owner and read by its owner at his or her leisure for escape, consolation, inspiration.

6. Along with its closure and reinforcement of patriarchy, the fairy tale also served to encourage notions of rags to riches, pull yourself up by your bootstraps, dreaming, miracles, and such.

7. There was always tension between the literary and oral traditions. The oral tales continued and continue to threaten the more conventional and classical tales because they can question, dislodge, and deconstruct the written tales. Moreover, within the literary tradition itself, there were numerous writers such as Charles Dickens, George MacDonald, Lewis Carroll, Oscar Wilde, and Edith Nesbit who questioned the standardized model of what a fairy tale should be.

8. It was through script that there was a full-scale debate about what oral folk tales and literary fairy tales were and what their respective functions should be. By the end of the nineteenth century, the fairy tale had expanded as a high art form (operas, ballets, dramas) and low art form (folk plays, vaudevilles, and parodies) and a form developed classically and experimentally for children and adults. The oral tales continued to be disseminated through communal gatherings of different kinds, but they were also broadcast by radio and gathered in books by folklorists. Most important in the late nineteenth century was the rise of folklore as an institution and various schools of literary criticism that dealt with fairy tales and folk tales.

9. Though many fairy-tale books and collections were illustrated and some lavishly illustrated in the nineteenth century the images were very much in conformity with the text. The illustrators were frequently anonymous and did not seem to count. Though the illustrations often enriched and deepened a tale, they were more subservient to the text.

However, the domination of the word in the development of the fairy tale as genre was about to change. The next great revolution in the institutionalization of the genre was the film, for the images now imposed themselves on the text and formed their own text in violation of print but also with the help of the print culture. And here is where Walt Disney and other animators enter the scene.

By the turn of the twentieth century there had already been a number of talented illustrators such as Gustav Doré, George Cruikshank, Walter Crane, Charles Folkard, and Arthur Rackham who had demonstrated great ingenuity in their interpretations of fairy tales through their images. In addition, the broadside, broadsheet, or *image d'Epinal* had spread in Europe and America during the latter part of the nineteenth century as a forerunner of the comic book, and these sheets with printed images and texts anticipated the first animated cartoons that were produced at the beginning of the twentieth century. Actually, the French filmmaker Georges Méliès began experimenting as early as 1896 with types of fantasy and fairy-tale motifs in his *féeries* or trick films.[1] He produced versions of *Cinderella, Bluebeard*, and *Red Riding Hood* among others. However, since the cinema industry itself was still in its early phase of development, it was difficult for Méliès to bring about a major change in the technological and cinematic institutionalization of the genre. As Lewis Jacobs has remarked, "this effort of Méliès illustrated rather than re-created the fairy tale. Yet, primitive though it was, the order of the scenes did form a coherent, logical, and progressive continuity. A new way of making moving pictures had been invented. Scenes could now be staged and selected specially for the camera, and the movie maker could control both the material and its arrangement."[2]

During the early part of the twentieth century Walter Booth, Anson Dyer, Lotte Reiniger, Walter Lantz, and others all used fairy-tale plots in different ways in trick films and cartoons, but none of the early animators ever matched the intensity with which Disney occupied himself with the fairy tale. In fact, it is noteworthy that Disney's very first endeavors in animation (not considering the advertising commercials he made) were the fairy-tale adaptations that he produced with Ub Iwerks in Kansas City between 1922-1923: *The Four Musicians of Bremen, Little Red Riding Hood, Puss in Boots, Jack and the Beanstalk, Goldie Locks and the Three Bears*, and *Cinderella*. To a certain degree, Disney identified so closely with the fairy tales he appropriated that it is no wonder his name virtually became synonymous with the genre of the fairy tale itself.

However, before discussing Disney's particular relationship to the fairy-tale tradition, it is important to consider the conditions of early animation in America and the role of the animator in general, for all this has a bearing on Disney's productive relationship with the fairy tale. In his important study, *Before Mickey: The Animated Film, 1898-1928*, Donald Crafton remarks that

the early animated film was the location of a process found elsewhere in cinema but nowhere else in such intense concentration: self-figuration, the tendency of the filmmaker to interject himself into his film. This can take several forms it can be direct or indirect, and more or less camouflaged. . . . At first it was obvious and literal; at the end it was subtle and cloaked in metaphors and symbolic imagery designed to facilitate the process and yet to keep the idea gratifying for the artist and the audience. Part of the animation game consisted of developing mythologies that gave the animator some sort of special status. Usually these were very flattering, for he was pictured as (or implied to be) a demigod, a purveyor of life itself.[3]

As Crafton convincingly shows, the early animators before Disney literally drew themselves into the pictures and often appeared as characters in the films. One of the more interesting aspects of the early animated films is a psychically loaded tension between the artist and the characters he drew, one that is ripe for a Freudian or Lacanian reading, for the artist is always threatening to take away their "lives," while they, in turn, seek to deprive him of his pen (phallus) or creative inspiration so that they can control their own lives. (Almost all the early animators were men, and their pens and camera work assume a distinctive phallic function in early animation.) The hand with pen or pencil is featured in many animated films in the process of creation, and it is then transformed in many films into the tails of a cat or dog. These tails then act as the productive force or artist's instrument throughout the film. For instance, Disney in his

Alice films often employed a cat named Julius, who would take off his tail and use it as stick, weapon, rope, hook, question mark, and so forth. It was the phallic means to induce action and conceive a way out of a predicament.

The celebration of the pen/phallus as ruler of the symbolic order of the film was in keeping with the way that animated films were actually produced in the studios during the 1920s. That is, most of the studios, largely located in New York, had become taylorized and were run by men who joined together under the supervision of the head of the studio to produce the cartoons. After making his first fairy-tale films in close cooperation with Ub Iwerks in Kansas City, Disney moved to Hollywood, where he developed the taylorized studio to the point of perfection. Under his direction, the films were carefully scripted to project his story or vision of how a story should be related. The story line was carried by hundreds of repetitious images created by the artists in his studios. Their contribution was in many respects like the dwarfs in *Snow White and the Seven Dwarfs*: they were to do the spadework, while the glorified prince was to come along and carry away the prize.

It might be considered somewhat one-dimensional to examine all of Disney's films as self-figurations, or embodiments of the chief designer's[4] wishes and beliefs. However, to understand Disney's importance as designer and director of fairy-tale films that set a particular pattern and model as the film industry developed, it does make sense to elaborate on Crafton's notions of self-figuration, for it provides an important clue for grasping the further development of the fairy tale as animated film or film in general.

We have already seen that one of the results stemming from the shift from the oral to the literary in the institutionalization of the fairy tale was a loss of live contact with the storyteller and a sense of community or commonality. This loss was a result of the social-industrial transformations at the end of the nineteenth century with the *Gem-*

einschaft (community) giving way to the *Gesellschaft* (society). However, it was not a total loss, for industrialization brought about greater comfort, sophistication, and literacy and new kinds of communication in public institutions. Therefore, as I have demonstrated, the literary fairy tale's ascent corresponded to violent and progressive shifts in society and celebrated individualism, subjectivity, and reflection. It featured the narrative voice of the educated author and publisher over communal voices and set new guidelines for freedom of speech and expression. In addition, proprietary rights to a particular tale were established, and the literary tale became a commodity that paradoxically spoke out in the name of the unbridled imagination. Indeed, because it was born out of alienation, the literary fairy tale fostered a search for new "magical" means to overcome the instrumentalization of the imagination.

By 1900 literature began to be superseded by the mechanical means of reproduction that, Walter Benjamin declared, were revolutionary: "the technique of reproduction detaches the reproduced object from the domain of tradition. By making many reproductions it substitutes a plurality of copies of a unique existence. And in permitting the reproduction to meet the beholder or listener in his own particular situation, it reactivates the object reproduced. These two processes lead to a tremendous shattering of tradition which is the obverse of the contemporary crisis and renewal of mankind. Both processes are intimately connected with the contemporary mass movements. Their most powerful agent is the film. Its social significance, particularly in its most positive form, is inconceivable without its destructive, cathartic aspect, that is, the liquidation of the traditional value of the cultural heritage."[5] Benjamin analyzed how the revolutionary technological nature of the film could either bring about an aestheticization of politics leading to the violation of the masses through fascism, or a politicization of aesthetics that provides the necessary critical detachment for the masses to take charge of their own destiny.

In the case of the fairy-tale film at the beginning of the twentieth century, there are "revolutionary" aspects that we can note, and they prepared the way for progressive innovation that expanded the horizons of viewers and led to greater understanding of social conditions and culture. But there were also regressive uses of mechanical reproduction that brought about the cult of the personality and commodification of film narratives. For instance, the voice in fairy-tale films is at first effaced so that the image totally dominates the screen, and the words or narrative voice can only speak through the designs of the animator who, in the case of Walt Disney, has signed his name prominently on the screen. In fact, for a long time, Disney did not give credit to the artists and technicians who worked on his films. These images were intended both to smash the aura of heritage and to celebrate the ingenuity, inventiveness, and genius of the animator. In most of the early animated films, there were few original plots, and the story lines did not count. Most important were the gags, or the technical inventions of the animators, ranging from introducing live actors to interact with cartoon characters to improving the movement of the characters so that they did not shimmer to devising ludicrous and preposterous scenes for the sake of spectacle. It did not matter what story was projected so long as the images astounded the audience, captured its imagination for a short period of time, and left the people laughing or staring in wonderment. The purpose of the early animated films was to make audiences awestruck and to celebrate the magical talents of the animator as demigod. As a result, the fairy tale as story was a vehicle for animators to express their artistic talents and develop the technology. The animators sought to impress audiences with their abilities to use pictures in such a way that they would forget the earlier fairy tales and remember the images that they, the new artists, were creating for them.

Through these moving pictures, the animators appropriated literary and oral fairy tales to subsume the word, to have the final word, often through image and book, for Disney began publishing books during the 1930s to complement his films.

Of all the early animators, Disney was the one who truly revolutionized the fairy tale as institution through the cinema. One could almost say that he was obsessed by the fairy-tale genre, or, put another way, Disney felt drawn to fairy tales because they reflected his own struggles in life. After all, Disney came from a relatively poor family, suffered from the exploitative and stern treatment of an unaffectionate father, was spurned by his early sweetheart, and became a success due to his tenacity, cunning, and courage and his ability to gather talented artists and managers like his brother Roy around him.

One of his early films, *Puss in Boots*, is crucial for grasping his approach to the literary fairy tale and for understanding how he used it as self-figuration that would mark the genre for years to come. Disney did not especially care whether one knew the original Perrault text of *Puss in Boots* or some other popular version. It is also unclear which text he actually knew. However, what is clear is that Disney sought to replace all versions with his animated version and that his cartoon is astonishingly autobiographical.

If we recall, Perrault wrote his tale in 1697 to reflect upon a cunning cat whose life is threatened and who manages to survive by using his brains to trick a king and an ogre. On a symbolical level, the cat represented Perrault's conception of the role of the haute bourgeoisie (his own class), who comprised the administrative class of Louis XIV's court and who were often the mediators between the peasantry and aristocracy. Of course, there are numerous ways to read Perrault's tale, but whatever approach one chooses, it is apparent that the major protagonist is the cat.

This is not the case in Disney's film. The hero is a young man, a commoner, who is in love with the king's daughter, and she fondly returns his affection. At the same time, the hero's black cat, a female, is having a romance with the royal white cat, who is the king's chauffeur. When the gigantic king discovers that the young man is wooing his daughter, he kicks him out of the palace, followed by Puss. At first, the hero does not want Puss's help, nor will he buy her the boots that she sees in a shop window. Then they go to the movies together and see a film with "Rudolph Vaselino" as a bull-fighter that spurs the imagination of Puss. Consequently, she tells the hero that she now has an idea which will help him win the king's daughter, providing that he will buy her the boots.

Of course, the hero will do anything to obtain the king's daughter. Puss explains to him that he must disguise himself as a masked bullfighter, and she will use a hypnotic machine behind the scenes so he can defeat the bull and win the approval of the king. When the day of the bullfight arrives, the masked hero struggles but eventually manages to defeat the bull. The king is so overwhelmed by his performance that he offers his daughter's hand in marriage, but first he wants to know who the masked champion is. When the hero reveals himself, the king is enraged, but the hero grabs the princess and leads her to the king's chauffeur. The white cat jumps in front with Puss, and they speed off with the king vainly chasing after them.

Although Puss as cunning cat is crucial in this film, Disney focuses most of his attention on the young man who wants to succeed at all costs. In contrast to the traditional fairy tale, the hero is not a peasant, nor is he dumb. Read as a "parable" of Disney's life at that moment, the hero can be seen as young Disney wanting to break into the industry of animated films (the king) with the help of Ub Iwerks (Puss). The hero upsets the king and runs off with his prize possession. Thus, the king is dispossessed, and the young man outraces him with the help of his friends.

But Disney's film is also an attack on the literary tradition of the fairy tale. He robs the literary tale of its voice and changes its form and meaning. Since the cinematic medium is a popular form of expression and accessible to the public at large, Disney actually returns the fairy tale to the majority of people. The images (scenes, frames, characters, gestures, jokes) are readily comprehensible for young and old alike from different social classes. In fact, the fairy tale is practically infantilized, just as the jokes are infantile. The plot records the deepest oedipal desire of every young boy: the son humiliates and undermines the father and runs off with his most valued object of love, the daughter/wife. By simplifying this complex semiotically in black and white drawings and making fun of it so that it had a common appeal, Disney also touched on other themes:

1. Democracy: The film is very *American* in its attitude toward royalty. The monarchy is debunked, and a commoner causes a kind of revolution.

2. Technology: It is through the new technological medium of the movies that Puss's mind is stimulated. Then she uses a hypnotic machine to defeat the bull and another fairly new invention, the automobile, to escape the king.

3. Modernity: The setting is obviously the twentieth century, and the modern minds are replacing the ancient. The revolution takes place as the king is outpaced and will be replaced by a commoner who knows how to use the latest inventions.

But who is this commoner? Was Disney making a statement on behalf of the masses? Was Disney celebrating "everyone" or "every man"? Did Disney believe in revolution and social change in the name of socialism? The answer to all these questions is simply—no.

Disney's hero is the enterprising young man, the entrepreneur who uses technology to his advantage. He does nothing to help the people or the community. In fact, he deceives the masses and the king by creating the illusion that he is stronger than the bull. He has learned, with the

help of Puss, that one can achieve glory through deception.
It is through the artful uses of images that one can sway
audiences and gain their favor. Animation is trickery—trick
films—for still images are made to seem as if they move
through automatization. As long as one controls the images
(and machines) one can reign supreme, just as the hero is
safe as long as he is disguised. The pictures conceal the controls and machinery. They deprive the audience of viewing
the production and manipulation, and in the end, audiences
can no longer envision a fairy tale for themselves as they
can when they read it. The pictures deprive the audience
now of visualizing their own characters, roles, and desires.
At the same time, Disney offsets the deprivation with the
pleasure of scopophilia and inundates the viewer with delightful images, humorous figures, and erotic signs. In general, the animator, Disney, projects the enjoyable fairy tale
of his life through his own images, and he realizes through
animated stills his basic oedipal dream that he was to play
out time and again in most of his fairy-tale films. It is the
repetition of Disney's infantile quest—the core of American
mythology—that enabled him to strike a chord in American
viewers from the 1920s to the present.

However, it was not through *Puss in Boots* and his other
early animated fairy tales that he was to captivate audiences
and set the "classical" modern model for animated fairy-
tale films. They were just the beginning. Rather, it was in
Snow White and the Seven Dwarfs that Disney fully appropriated the literary fairy-tale and made his signature into a
trademark for the most acceptable type of fairy tale in the
twentieth century. But before the making of *Snow White*,
there were important developments in his life and in the
film industry that illustrate why and how *Snow White* became the first definitive animated fairy-tale film—definitive
in the sense that it was to define the way other animated
films in the genre of the fairy tale were to be made.

After Disney had made several Laugh-O-Gram fairy-tale

films, all ironic and modern interpretations of the classical versions, he moved to Hollywood in 1923 and was successful in producing 56 *Alice* films, which involved a young pubescent girl in different adventures with cartoon characters. By 1927 these films were no longer popular, so he and Ub Iwerks developed Oswald the Lucky Rabbit cartoons that also found favor with audiences. However, in February of 1928, while Disney was in New York trying to renegotiate a contract with his distributor Charles Mintz, he learned that Mintz, who owned the copyright to Oswald, had lured some of Disney's best animators to work for another studio. Disney faced bankruptcy because he refused to capitulate to the exploitative conditions that Mintz set for the distribution and production of Disney's films.[6] This experience sobered Disney in his attitude toward the cutthroat competition in the film industry, and when he returned to Hollywood, he vowed to maintain complete control over all his productions—a vow that he never broke.

In the meantime, he and Iwerks had to devise another character for their company if they were to survive, and they conceived the idea for films featuring a pert mouse named Mickey. By September of 1928, after making two Mickey Mouse shorts, Disney, similar to his masked champion in *Puss in Boots*, had devised a way to gain revenge on Mintz and other animation studios by producing the first animated cartoon with sound, *Steamboat Willie*, starring Mickey Mouse. From this point on, Disney became known for introducing all kinds of new inventions and improving animation so that animated films became almost as realistic as films with live actors and natural settings. His next step after sound was color, and in 1932 he signed an exclusive contract with Technicolor and began producing his *Silly Symphony Cartoons* in color. More important, Disney released *The Three Little Pigs* in 1933 and followed it with *The Big Bad Wolf* and *The Three Little Wolves*, all of which involved fairy-tale characters and stories that touched on the lives of

people during the depression, for as Bob Thomas has re-
marked, "*The Three Little Pigs* was acclaimed by the Nation.
The wolf was on many American doorsteps, and 'Who's
Afraid of the Big Bad Wolf?' became a rallying cry."[7]

Not only were wolves on the doorsteps of Americans but
also witches, and to a certain extent, Disney with the help
of his brother Roy and Iwerks, had been keeping "evil" con-
nivers and competitors from the entrance to the Disney Studios throughout the 1920s. Therefore, it is not by chance
that Disney's next major experiment would involve a banished princess, loved by a charming prince, who would triumph over deceit and regain the rights to her castle. *Snow
White and the Seven Dwarfs* was to bring together all the
personal strands of Disney's own story with the destinies of
desperate Americans, who sought hope and solidarity in
their fight for survival during the Depression of the 1930s.

Of course, by 1934 Disney was, comparatively speaking,
wealthy, and now that he had money and had hired Don
Graham, a professional artist, to train his own animators at
the Disney Art School, founded in November 1932, he
could embark on ventures to stun moviegoers with his ingenuity and talents as organizer, storyteller, and filmmaker.
Conceived sometime in 1934, *Snow White* was to take three
years to complete, and Disney did not leave one stone un-
turned in his preparations for the first full-length animated
fairy-tale film ever made in history. Disney knew he was
making history.

During the course of the next three years, Disney worked
closely with all the animators and technicians assigned to the
production of *Snow White*. By now, Disney had divided his
studio into numerous departments such as animation, lay-
out, sound, music, and storytelling, and there were even sub-
divisions so that certain animators were placed in charge of
developing the characters of Snow White, the prince, the
dwarfs, and the queen/crone. Disney spent thousands of dol-
lars on a multiplane camera to capture the live action depic-

tions that he desired, the depth of the scenes, and close-ups. In addition he had his researchers experiment with colored gels, blurring focus, and filming through frosted glass, and he employed the latest inventions in sound and music to improve the synchronization with the characters on the screen. Throughout the entire production of this film, Disney had to be consulted and give his approval for each stage of development. After all, *Snow White* was his story that he had taken from the Grimm Brothers and changed completely to suit his tastes and beliefs. He cast a spell over this German tale and transformed it into something peculiarly American.

Just what were the changes he induced? In Disney's version, Snow White is an orphan. Neither her father nor her mother are alive, and she is at first depicted as a kind of Cinderella, cleaning the castle as a maid in a patched dress. In the Grimms' version there is the sentimental death of her mother. Her father remains alive, and she was never forced to do the work of commoners such as wash the steps of the castle. Also, Disney has the Prince appear at the very beginning of the film on a white horse and sing a song of love and devotion to Snow White, though he plays a negligible role in the Grimms' version. In the Disney film, the queen not only is jealous that Snow White is more beautiful than she is, but also sees the prince singing to Snow White and is envious because her stepdaughter has such a handsome suitor. Though the forest and the animals do not speak, they are anthromorphologized by Disney. In particular the animals befriend Snow White and become her protectors. Disney's dwarfs are hardworking and rich miners, and he gave them names—Doc, Sleepy, Bashful, Happy, Sneezy, Grumpy, Dopey—representative of certain human characteristics. His dwarfs are fleshed-out so that they become the star attractions of the film. Their actions are what counts in defeating evil. In the Grimms' tale, the dwarfs are anonymous and play a humble role. Disney's queen only comes to the cottage Snow White shares with the dwarfs one time

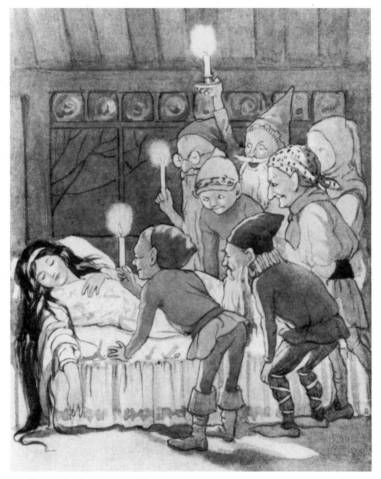

Illustration by Margaret Tarrant, 1936.

instead of three as in the Grimms' version, and she is killed
while trying to destroy the dwarfs by rolling a huge stone
down a mountain to crush them. The punishment in the
Grimms' tale is more horrifying: she must dance in red-hot
iron shoes at Snow White's wedding. Finally, Disney's Snow
White does not return to life when a dwarf stumbles while
carrying the glass coffin as in the Grimms' tale. She returns

to life when the prince, who has searched far and wide for her, arrives and bestows a kiss on her lips. His kiss of love is the only antidote to the queen's poison.

At first glance, it would seem that the changes that Disney made were not momentous. If we recall Sandra Gilbert and Susan Gubar's stimulating analysis in their book, *The Madwoman in the Attic*,[8] the film follows the classic "sexist" narrative about the framing of women's lives through a male discourse. Such male framing drives women to frustration and some women to the point of madness. It also pits women against women in competition for male approval (the mirror) of their beauty that is short-lived. No matter what they may do, women cannot chart their own lives without male manipulation and intervention, and in the Disney film, the prince plays even more of a framing role since he is introduced at the beginning while Snow White is singing, "I'm Wishing for the One I Love To Find Me Today." He will also appear at the end as the fulfillment of her dreams.

There is no doubt that Disney retained key ideological features of the Grimms' fairy tale that reinforce nineteenth-century patriarchal notions which Disney shared with the Grimms. In some way, he can even be considered their descendant, for he preserves and carries on many of their benevolent attitudes toward women. For instance, in the Grimms' tale, when Snow White arrives at the cabin, she pleads with the dwarfs to allow her to remain and promises that she will wash the dishes, mend their clothes, and clean the house. In Disney's film, she arrives and notices that the house is dirty. So, she convinces the animals to help her make the cottage tidy so that the dwarfs will perhaps let her stay there. Of course, the house for the Grimms and Disney was the place where good girls remained, and one aspect of the fairy tale and the film is about the domestication of women.

However, Disney went much further than the Grimms to make his film more memorable than the tale, for he does not celebrate the domestication of women so much as the triumph of the banished and the underdogs. That is, he celebrates his destiny, and insofar as he had shared marginal status with many Americans, he also celebrated an American myth of Horatio Alger: it is a male myth about perseverance, hard work, dedication, loyalty, and justice.

It may seem strange to argue that Disney perpetuated a male myth through his fairy-tale films when, with the exception of *Pinocchio*, they all featured young women as "heroines." However, despite their beauty and charm, Sleeping Beauty, Cinderella, and the other heroines are pale and pathetic compared to the more active and demonic characters in the film. The witches are not only agents of evil but represent erotic and subversive forces that are more appealing both for the artists who drew them and for the audiences.[9] The young women are like helpless ornaments in need of protection, and when it comes to the action of the film, they are omitted.

In *Snow White and the Seven Dwarfs*, the film does not really become lively until the dwarfs enter the narrative. They are the mysterious characters who inhabit a cottage, and it is through their hard work and solidarity that they are able to maintain a world of justice and restore harmony to the world. The dwarfs can be interpreted as the humble American workers, who pull together during a depression. They keep their spirits up by singing a song, "Hi Ho, it's home from work we go," or "Hi Ho, it's off to work we go," and their determination is the determination of every worker, who will succeed just as long as he does his share while women stay at home and keep the house clean. Of course, it is also possible to see the workers as Disney's own employees, on whom he depended for the glorious outcome of his films. In this regard, the prince can be interpreted as Disney, who directed the love story from the beginning. If we recall, it is the prince who frames the narrative. He announces his great love at the beginning of the film, and

Snow White cannot be fulfilled until he arrives to kiss her. During the major action of the film, he, like Disney, is lurking in the background and waiting for the proper time to make himself known. When he does arrive, he takes all the credit as champion of the disenfranchised, and he takes Snow White to his castle while the dwarfs are left as keepers of the forest.

But what has the prince actually done to deserve all the credit? What did Disney actually do to have his name flash on top of the title—"Walt Disney's *Snow White and the Seven Dwarfs*"—in big letters and later credit his co-workers in small letters? Disney never liked to give credit to the animators who worked with him, and they had to fight for acknowledgment. Disney always made it clear that he was the boss and owned total rights to his products. He himself had struggled for his independence against his greedy and unjust father and against fierce and ruthless competitors in the film industry. As producer of the fairy-tale films and major owner of the Disney studios, he wanted to figure in the film, and he sought, as Crafton has noted, to create a more indelible means of self-figuration. He accomplished this by stamping his signature as owner on the frame with the title of the film and then by having himself embodied in the figure of the prince. It is the prince Disney who made inanimate figures come to life through his animated films, and it is the prince who is to be glorified in *Snow White and the Seven Dwarfs* when he resuscitates the heroine with a magic kiss. Afterwards he holds Snow White in his arms, and in the final frame, he leads her off on a white horse to his golden castle on a hill. His golden castle—every woman's dream—supersedes the dark, sinister castle of the queen. The prince becomes her reward, and his power and wealth are glorified in the end.

There are obviously mixed messages or multiple messages in *Snow White and the Seven Dwarfs*, but the overriding sign, in my estimation, is the signature of Disney's self-

Illustration by Margaret Tarrant, 1936.

glorification in the name of justice. Disney wants the world *cleaned up*, and the pastel colors with their sharply drawn ink lines create images of cleanliness, just as each sequence reflects a clearly conceived and preordained destiny for all the characters in the film. For Disney, the Grimms' tale is not a vehicle to explore the deeper implications of the narrative and its history.[10] Rather, it is a vehicle to display what he can do as an animator with the latest technological and artistic developments in the industry. The story is secondary, and if there is a major change in the plot, it centers on the power of the prince, the only one who can save Snow White, and he becomes the focal point by the end of the story.

In Disney's early work with fairy tales in Kansas City, he had a wry and irreverent attitude toward the classical narratives, and there was a strong suggestion in the manner in which he and Iwerks rewrote and filmed the tales that they were "revolutionaries," the new boys on the block, who were about to introduce innovative methods of animation into the film industry and speak for the outcasts. However, in 1934, Disney is already the kingpin of animation, and he uses all that he had learned to reinforce his power and command of fairy-tale animation. The manner in which he copied the musical plays and films of his time, and his close adaptation of fairy tales with patriarchal codes indicate that all the technical experiments would not be used to foster social change in America, but to keep power in the hands of individuals like himself, who felt empowered to design and create new worlds. As Richard Schickel has perceptively remarked, Disney "could make something his own, all right, but that process nearly always robbed the work at hand of its uniqueness, of its soul, if you will. In its place he put jokes and songs and fright effects, but he always seemed to diminish what he touched. He came always as a conqueror, never as a servant. It is a trait, as many have observed, that many Americans share when they venture into foreign lands hoping to do good but equipped only with knowhow instead of sympathy and respect for alien traditions."[11]

Disney always wanted to do something new and unique just as long as he had absolute control. He also knew that novelty would depend on the collective skills of his employees, whom he had to keep happy or indebted to him in some way. Therefore, from 1934 onward, about the time that he conceived his first feature-length fairy-tale film, Disney became the orchestrator of a corporate network that changed the function of the fairy-tale genre in America. The power of Disney's fairy-tale films does not reside in the uniqueness or novelty of the productions, but in Disney's great talent for holding antiquated views of society *still* through animation and his use of the latest technological developments in cinema to his advantage.

Disney's adaptation of the literary fairy tale for the screen led to a number of changes in the institution of the genre. Technique now takes precedence over the story, and the story is used to celebrate the technician and his means. The carefully arranged images narrate through seduction and imposition of the animator's hand and the camera. The images and sequences engender a sense of wholeness, seamless totality, and harmony that is orchestrated by a savior/technician on and off the screen. Though the characters are fleshed out to become more realistic, they are also one-dimensional and are to serve functions in the film. There is no character development because the characters are stereotypes, arranged according to a credo of domestication of the imagination. The domestication is related to colonization insofar as the ideas and types are portrayed as models of behavior to be emulated. Exported through the screen as models, the "American" fairy tale colonizes other national audiences. What is good for Disney is good for the world, and what is good in a Disney fairy tale is good in the rest of the world. The thematic emphasis on cleanliness, control, and organized industry reinforces the technics of the film itself: the clean frames with attention paid to every detail; the precise drawing and manipulation of the characters as real people; the careful plotting of the events that focus on salvation through the male hero. Private reading pleasure is replaced by pleasurable viewing in an impersonal cinema. Here one is brought together with other viewers not for the development of community but to be diverted in the French sense of *divertissement* and American sense of diversion. The diversion of the Disney fairy tale is geared toward nonreflective viewing. Everything is on the surface, one-dimensional, and we are to delight in one-dimensional portrayal and thinking, for it is adorable, easy, and comforting in its simplicity.

Once Disney realized how successful he was with his formula for feature-length fairy tales, he never abandoned it, and in fact, if one regards two recent Disney Studio productions, *Beauty and the Beast* and *Aladdin*, Disney's contemporary animators have continued in his footsteps. There is nothing but the "eternal return of the same" in *Beauty and the Beast* and *Aladdin* that makes for enjoyable viewing and delight in techniques of these films as commodities but nothing new in the exploration of narration, animation, and signification.

There is something sad in the manner in which Disney "violated" the literary genre of the fairy tale and packaged his versions in his name through the merchandising of all sorts of books, articles, clothing, and records. Instead of using technology to enhance the communal aspects of narrative and bring about major changes in viewing stories to stir and animate viewers, he employed animators and technology to stop thinking about change, to return to his films, and to long nostalgically for neatly ordered patriarchal realms. Fortunately, the animation of the literary fairy tale did not stop with Disney, but that is another tale to tell, a tale about breaking Disney's magic spell.

4. SPREADING MYTHS ABOUT IRON JOHN

When I first heard the title of Robert Bly's book about men, *Iron John*, I made several quick associations[1]: man of steel, superman, invincible force, solid, but flying through the air faster than a speeding bullet. Explosive. The savior. Reliable. Law and order. John, not Jack. Formality. The Christian John. Stiff. Cold. Inhibited. Not Johnnie. Not Jock. John the Baptist. John the Apostle. Onward Christian soldiers. Blood and iron. Bismarck. Germany. War.

Never could John be wild. Perhaps Johnny. Perhaps Jack. There was definitely something noble and heroic about the name Iron John, like the kings, dubbed with names signifying their outstanding traits: Richard the Lion-Hearted, Louis the Sun King, Frederick the Great. *Iron John* was clearly a book about proud strong men, about great men, sovereign stoic studs.

On the contrary. My associations were wrong. *Iron John*, I discovered, was not about old legendary heroes but about the new meek men of today who desperately need to get in touch with that inner iron stuff from which mythical Iron Johns are made. More precisely, Bly's book is about *American* soft men, whom he wants to train and run through a rigorous initiatory path in eight stages that he gleans from a *German* fairy tale, *Der Eisenhans* or *Iron Hans*, published by Wilhelm Grimm in 1850. The adventures in this tale are

Illustration by Otto Ubbelohde, 1922.

thus paradigmatic metaphors and provide a healing process for American men, whose relations to their fathers have deteriorated because of the demands of industrialization, and who have been led astray by the women's movement. Confused about their identity, American men must learn the true meaning of what it is to be wild, to overcome their malaise and complete their journeys of male self-realization. Bly makes an important distinction between savage and wild so that readers will not be confused about what today's confused males need, but before I discuss this distinction and the problems that I have with his mythopoetic diagnosis of the sufferings of contemporary American men, let me briefly recount the plot of *Iron Hans* so that we can grasp why Bly has focused on this particular tale to expound his psycho-philosophical notions about wildness and maleness.

Wilhelm Grimm's version, *Iron Hans*, features a king

whose forest is inhabited by some mysterious creature who kills all who enter it. For many years nobody ventures into the forest until a stranger arrives and disenchants the forest by capturing a wild man, who had been dwelling in a deep pool. This man was brown as rusty iron, and his hair hung over his face down to his knees. The king has the wild man placed in an iron cage in the castle courtyard, gives the key to the cage to the queen, and forbids anyone to open it under the penalty of death. However, one day the king's eight-year-old son loses his golden ball, and it bounces into the cage. So, the wild man tells him that the only way he can regain his ball is by stealing the key from under his mother's pillow and opening the cage. When the boy finally frees the wild man, he is so terrified of his father's wrath that he asks the wild man to take him along.

The wild man carries the boy to a golden spring in the forest and tells him that he must not allow anything to fall into it or else the water will become polluted. However, the boy's finger, which had gotten stuck while he was freeing the wild man, begins to hurt, and he dips it into the spring. The finger turns to gold, as does his hair after the wild man gives him two more chances. Therefore, the boy must leave the forest. But the wild man reveals his name to the boy and tells him that whenever he needs something he is to return to the forest and cry out "Iron Hans."

The prince covers his golden hair with a little cap and eventually obtains a job as a gardener's helper at another king's castle. One day, while working in the garden, he takes off his cap, and the king's daughter notices his golden hair from her window. She invites him to her room and rewards him for bringing flowers to her. Soon after this, with the help of Iron John, who gives him a magnificent steed and knights, the boy helps the king win a war. Disguised in armor, he leads a troop of knights into battle and then disappears quickly, returning the stallion and knights to Iron Hans to resume working as the simple gardener's helper.

Illustration by Otto Ubbelohde, 1922.

In order to discover the strange knight's identity, the king holds a tournament. The princess throws out a golden apple three days in a row, and the disguised prince, helped by Iron Hans, who gives him red, white, and black armors and horses, rides off with the prize each time. However, on the third day, the king's men give pursuit and manage to wound him and catch a glimpse of his golden hair before he escapes. The next day, the princess asks her father to summon the gardener's helper, and she reveals his golden hair. Consequently, he produces the golden apples to show that he was indeed the true hero of the tournament. As a reward, the young man asks to marry the princess, and on the wedding day, his mother and father attend and are filled with joy. During the celebration, Iron Hans suddenly appears, embraces the bridegroom, and says, "I am Iron Hans and was turned into a wild man by a magic spell. But you released me from the spell, and now all the treasures that I possess shall be yours."[2]

So much for the 1850 Grimm version of *Iron Hans*. As I have already noted, the Bly interpretation of 1990 is based on a premise that there is a wild man in each of us males that we must recuperate if we are to become vigorous and understand who we are; that is, there is almost a categorical imperative for males to become Iron Johns, or else we shall never know our authentic maleness. As he suggests, "every modern male has, lying at the bottom of his psyche, a large, primitive being covered with hair down to his feet. Making contact with this Wild Man is the step the Eighties male or the Nineties male has yet to take. That bucketing-out process has yet to begin in our contemporary culture."[3] For Bly, American men have undergone generational changes without their basic psychic structure having been disturbed. But the contact to what is at the bottom of every male psyche has been severed. For instance, in the 1950s, men were allegedly confident about their virile powers and identified themselves with aggression, toughness, and power. This one-sided identity began to weaken during the Vietnam War, and in reaction to the lies, deceit, and murder of that period, American men began nurturing their feminine side and eventually became too soft.

Though Bly recognizes a positive side in this development—men are more gentle, not interested in harming the earth or the stars—the American man, or rather, boy, lacks vitality and resolve. American men are not happy because they act to please not themselves but their mothers or their wives and lovers. Somehow they have not completed a journey which will lead them to the primitive in their soul, which Bly equates with the wild man. Hence, his choice of Wilhelm Grimm's tale, which he divides into eight segments so that his male readers can readily learn the steps they must take to grasp what it means to be wild.

In Bly's reconstruction of *Iron Hans*, Phase One, "The Pillow and the Key," is the onset of the journey that the boy must make to establish contact with the wild man within him. Important here is that the boy, to become a man, must break with the mother by stealing the key, and he must separate from both parents to test himself alone. Once in the forest, the second phase, "When One's Hair Turns Gold," begins, and it involves overcoming a childhood wound:

The ancient practice of initiation then—still very much alive in our genetic structure—offers a third way through, between two "natural" roads of manic excitement and victim excitement. A mentor or "male mother" enters the landscape. Behind him, a being of impersonal intensity stands, which in our story is the Wild Man, or Iron John. The young man investigates or experiences his wound—father wound, mother wound, or shaming-wound—in the presence of this independent, timeless mythological initiatory being.

If the young man steals the key and climbs on the shoulders of this being, three things will change: the wound, rather, than being regarded as bad luck, will be seen as a gift. Second, the sacred or secret water—whatever that is—will appear. Finally, the energy of the sun will somehow be carried into the man's body (36).

Now that the young man has a glimpse of his great potential, his mentor, the wild man, can send him into the world to realize what his golden talents are. This third phase, "The Road of Ashes, Descent and Grief," however,

begins with a fall or katabasis. The young man must learn
to do nitty-gritty work, experience humiliation, and disci-
pline himself to face the rigors of life. As he goes through
this phase, he also develops a yearning for a new father, and
the fourth phase, "The Hunger for the King in a Time with
No Father," commences. This corresponds to the psychological need to build up the generous and blessed side of the
father after dealing with the negative and destructive side of
the father.

Once the ideal father has been located, the fifth phase,
"The Meeting with the God-Woman in the Garden," takes
place. Here the young man in his twenties and thirties learns
to become a lover, but he must be careful about showing his
talents, his golden hair, to the woman and retain what he
needs for himself. At this point in the young man's development, it is necessary that he demonstrate his mettle as a
warrior, and in the sixth phase, "To Bring the Interior War-
riors Back to Life," Bly argues that there is a distinction
between a soldier, who is a murderer, and a true warrior,
who is a defender of his integrity and soul house. "Warrior-
ship inside, then, amounts to a soul alertness that helps protect a human being from being turned into copper wire, and
protects us from shamers, unconscious swordsmen, hostile
people, and greedy interior beings" (179).

Thus, when the king's country is invaded, the young
man, who identifies with this king, his daughter, and the
kingdom, rises to the occasion with the help of his mentor.
But the victory in battle does not complete the initiation. In
the seventh phase, "Riding the Red, the White and the
Black Horses," the young man needs time to modulate out of
the warrior mode through display, form, and ritual. Once this
is done in the tournament, the young man is ready for the
final phase, "The Wound by the King's Men," which symbolizes for Bly the memory of a primeval wound, grief, and the
womb within the male body. Without this wound as memory,
the young man cannot move to adulthood, establish contact

Illustration by John B. Gruelle, 1914.

with the wild man, and marry. As Bly concludes, "The Wild Man is the door to the wilderness in nature, but we could also say the Wild Man is nature itself. . . . The Wild Man encourages and amounts to a trust in what is below. . . . The Wild Man can only come to full life inside when the man has gone through the serious disciplines suggested by taking the first wound, doing kitchen and ashes work, creating a garden, bringing wild flowers to the Holy Woman, experiencing the warrior, riding the red, the white, and the black horses, learning to create art, and receiving the second heart" (224-25).

Through his choice of *Iron Hans* and his rereading the Grimm fairy tale as a kind of initiatory universal myth, Bly has created a new myth named *Iron John*, which he hopes will enable American men to understand the grief and terror they have been experiencing during the past twenty years or so and to regain pride in themselves and, as a consequence, in the American nation. In this regard, *Iron John* is a contemporary American myth, that wants to celebrate how men can regain their self-respect and become soulful leaders of their nation. Yet, despite Bly's noble intentions, his Jungian revision of *Iron Hans* cannot but lead male (and female) readers to have a distorted view of men and their potential to save themselves and become the great saviors of American culture. Moreover, Bly's interpretation of Wilhelm Grimm's *Iron Hans* is a folklorist's nightmare. In fact, his mythopoetic projections and dilettante references to myth and folklore obscure the origins and significance of *Iron Hans*, while his eclectic reconstruction of putative initiation rituals has more to do with his own yearning for a male mentor or his desire to become a male guru than with providing a rigorous analysis of the problems facing men in contemporary America. Certainly, it does not provide a viable means for discerning and dealing with them. To say the least, there is something pompous and self-serving in Bly's stylized self-reflection of the mythical Iron John that indicates, despite Bly's constant protestations to the contrary, that he too is part of the backlash against the women's movement, and what may be a nightmare for folklorists may also be a nightmare for American readers in general.

Iron John as nightmare. There is much to unravel in Bly's book: the fairy tale as myth, the myth as our story, our story as initiation and salvation, the salvation as nightmare. And, like any good nightmare, we must come to terms with its hidden meanings if we are to overcome our fear. So let us be like that hero whom Bly admires and who ventured forth to learn what fear was and try to discover what lies at the bottom of *Iron John* as nightmare.

At the beginning of his book, Bly maintains that *Iron Hans* was first set down by the Grimm brothers around 1820, but it could be ten or twenty thousand years old (5). At another point, he declares, "our story is not anti-Christian but pre-Christian by a thousand years or so" (8). Then he tells us that "the Iron John story, which is pre-Greek, does not polarize earth and sky" (43). Later he states that "our story is probably pre-Christian by several centuries" (208). All these assertions are misleading and need clarification.

Calling *Iron John* "our story" is a rhetorical device used to make readers believe that we have played a role in this story. Either it is part of our collective unconscious, part of our civilization and heritage, or part of own creative needs. Whatever the case may be, we are to assume that this story is our story, when it is clearly Bly narrating and blurring all narrative and historical distinctions. Even when Bly asserts that he, in his skewed translation of Wilhelm Grimm's *Iron John*, is recounting a tale from the Grimm Brothers that is probably thousands of years ago, he is falsifying history and creating his own myth.

Neither *Iron John* nor *Iron Hans* is *our* story. And neither *Iron John* nor *Iron Hans* is pre-Greek or pre-Christian. If we start by analyzing the historical origins of the text published by the Brothers Grimm, we shall discover some startling facts that shed light on the magical wand of Bly the mythmaker and compel us to question all the assumptions about maleness and storytelling in his book.

In 1815, the Brothers Grimm published a tale entitled *De wilde Mann (The Wild Man)* in dialect that they had obtained from a member of the aristocratic family von Haxthausen.[4] In brief, this tale concerns a wild man who was under a spell and constantly destroyed the fields of some peasants. Their king offered a reward for his capture, and when this demonic creature is lured into captivity by means of beer, he is locked in a cage. As in *Iron Hans*, the king's son loses his ball and must steal the key from his mother's pocket if he is to recover the ball. Once he does this and frees the wild man, he goes to the woods with the man because he is afraid of punishment by his father. Soon thereafter the wild man gives him a coarse coat and sends him to work at the emperor's garden as an assistant to the gardener. Each morning the wild man meets him in the garden and says, "now wash yourself and now comb yourself."[5] Immediately thereafter the boy becomes handsome, and the wild man makes the garden beautiful. The princess becomes attracted to the gardener's assistant, and after three meetings, they marry in secret. When her parents discover this, they make her work in the brewery, and she also has to support herself by spinning. The young man goes to work in the kitchen and helps the cook prepare the dinners. Sometimes he steals a piece of meat and brings it to his wife. At one point war erupts with England, and the emperor and his armies invade England. The young man procures a three-legged horse from a stable to set out for the war and requests aid from the wild man, who gives him a magnificent horse and a regiment of soldiers. The young man wins the battle for the emperor and refuses to tell the emperor who he is. Then he returns the horse and regiment to the wild man.

After this event, the young man helps the emperor two more times. On the last occasion, after the English are totally defeated, the young man is wounded, and the emperor wraps his own kerchief around the wound. Once they are all back at the emperor's court, the young man, disguised again as gardener's assistant, tells the emperor that if he hadn't been with him, it would not have turned out so well. The emperor wants to give him a beating, but then the young man reveals the wound and the kerchief. The emperor is amazed, begs his pardon, and gives him a kingdom. Once this occurs, the wild man is released from the magic spell, and it turns out that he was a great king. The mountain in which he was living turns into a royal castle, and the young man and his wife go to live with him until the end of their days.

The Brothers Grimm kept publishing this tale in a number of editions of the *Children and Household Tales (Kinder- und Hausmärchen)* until 1843. Then they eliminated it in favor of *Iron Hans*, a tale which Wilhelm Grimm virtually wrote by himself using the dialect version of *The Wild Man*, another oral story that they had collected from a member of the Hassenpflug family of Kassel, and a tale entitled *Der eiserne Hans (Iron Hans)* from Friedmund von Arnim's *100 neue Mährchen im Gebirge gesammelt* (1844).

As is well known, the Brothers published seven editions of *Children and Household Tales* from 1812 to 1857, and they made numerous changes along the way, eliminating, adding, and revising the tales for an assortment of reasons. From 1819 on, Wilhelm, the younger brother, was almost exclusively in charge of the revisions, and quite often he would create his own tales by compiling and editing several different versions of a basic type. In the case of *Iron Hans*, which was first published in 1850, not 1820 as Bly has asserted, Wilhelm synthesized literary and oral versions that folklorists have traced to two basic tale types, 314 *(The Youth Transformed to a Horse*, also known as *Goldener* in German, or *The Golden-Haired Youth at a King's Court)* and 502 *(The Wild Man)* according to *The Types of the Folk-Tale* by Antti Aarne and Stith Thompson.[6] Because of the difficulty of tracing the oral tales and their origins throughout the world, Aarne and Thompson compiled a typology of folk tales that has enabled folklorists to trace the historical and geographical origins of oral narratives. Given the evidence we have from the Brothers Grimm, Wilhelm's *Iron*

Hans is mainly based on tales that stem from type 314, *The Golden-Haired Youth*. As usual, there is a debate among folklorists about the origins of this type. Some place the tale's creation in India, while others argue that it originated during the latter part of the Roman Empire. There can be no conclusive proof, unless manuscripts are found that document certain theses. However, almost all folklorists agree that, as far as Wilhelm Grimm's version is concerned, the major plot line and motifs of the tale were formed during the Middle Ages in Europe. Furthermore, they were strongly influenced by a literary tradition, in particular a twelfth-century romance entitled *Robert der Teufel (Robert the Devil)*, which gave rise to many different literary and oral versions in medieval Europe.[7]

In *Robert der Teufel*,[8] the Count Hubertus of Normandy and his wife become skeptical about God's powers because they cannot conceive a child. They lose their faith in the Almighty, and the wife says that she would accept a child even it it were provided by the Devil. Indeed, she gives birth to a son named Robert, who is possessed by the Devil and has extraordinary powers. No one can control him, and he cannot master himself. Soon he is known by the name of Robert the Devil. When he turns seventeen and is made a knight, he terrorizes the region and commits many crimes. However, all this changes when his mother tells him to kill her because she is so ashamed of him and herself. She reveals the story of his birth, and he decides to make a pilgrimage to Rome. A holy hermit tells him that he must live the life of a fool or madman as repentance for his crimes. So Robert travels to the emperor's court, where he acts the fool and lives with dogs. Only the emperor's daughter, who cannot speak, knows that Robert is someone other than who he pretends to be. After seven years, a treacherous seneschal attempts to overthrow the emperor with the help of the Saracens. God commands Robert to help the emperor and gives him white armor and a white horse. As a result, Robert saves the Holy Roman Empire, and the emperor's daughter reveals that he is the true savior when his identity is doubted. Eventually, Robert marries the emperor's daughter and returns to Normandy, where he and his wife give birth to a son named Richard.

As can be seen from this brief summary, this popular romance contains most of the important motifs and features that one can find in the Grimms' tale *Iron Hans*, and it is more than likely that *Iron Hans* is a blend of this Christian legendary material and medieval folk tales dealing with the golden-haired youth. In other words, *Iron Hans* does not owe a great debt to some mythical pre-Greek or pre-Christian tale, but it can very clearly be traced to an aristocratic literary tradition that contained pagan and Christian elements and to European folklore of the Middle Ages. In many respects, the tale bears similarity to an initiation process that a young aristocrat was expected to undergo in the European Middle Ages to become a warrior and a king. In *Types of the Folk-Tale*, Aarne and Thompson divide the tale according to seven motifs:

I. *In the Devil's Service*—a boy is sold to the devil in return for his services as godfather or for pay. Sometimes the boy just goes at a certain agreed-upon time to the devil's castle.

II. *The Forbidden Chamber*—the boy breaks the prohibition against entering a certain chamber and as a mark of disobedience his hair turns to gold.

III. *The Magic Horse*—the boy is commanded to care for certain horses, one of which he is to abuse, but which is enchanted.

IV. *The Obstacle Flight*—the boy flees on a magic horse, and as the devil approaches, he throws magic objects behind him which become obstacles in the pursuer's path.

V. *The Gardener's Disguise*—the hero covers his gold hair with a cap or cloth and claims that he has a scalded head. Then he takes service in the king's court as gardener. After the princess falls in love with him, they marry but are put in a pigsty to live.

VI. *Conquests*—with the magic horses' help he wins a tournament for three days in succession, but remains unknown until af-

ter the third, or he shows his prowess in battle as a dragon-slayer
or bringer of a magic-remedy for the king.

VII. *The Disenchantment*—the magic horse is disenchanted.

This capsular outline allows us to see several contradic-
tions in Bly's rambling interpretation of what he has desig-
nated as a primeval initiatory narrative. As noted, if there
are signs of an initiation, it has more to do with the affirma-
tion of an aristocratic rite of education than some holy pre-
Greek and pre-Christian ritual. Most important, however,
the wild man is not a mentor but a demonic figure, whom
the young man flees with the help of a magical horse, who
is actually an enchanted prince. The golden hair is a stigma
that indicates his disobedience but that also indicates he is
an aristocrat, who refuses to succumb to the devil. He flees
the devil on an animal of aristocratic rank. Later, he proves
his prowess without the help of the devil/wild man, but
with the help of a royal or likeminded aristocrat, i.e., the
horse.

Obviously, the tale type of *The Golden-Haired Youth* is
open to other interpretations, depending on the text or version that one uses.[10] However, what is not open to interpretation is the constant appearance of the motif, the *conflict* with the devil, which appears in and forms the starting
point of most of the tales that predate Wilhelm Grimm's
version of 1850. Here it is legitimate to ask why Wilhelm
turned the demonic wild man into a more noble savage,
who does indeed serve as a guiding force in *Iron Hans*. But,
I believe, the answer does not lie, as Bly might suggest, in
some primeval unconsciousness or genetic constitution of
men but in Wilhelm's disposition and own psychological
needs. Wilhelm lost his father when he was only ten years
old, and the quest for a father figure is a leitmotif that can
be traced in many of the tales that he revised. Therefore, it
could be strongly argued that the manner in which Grimm
reconstituted the tale of *Iron Hans* had a great deal to do

with his own longing for a mentor, and it also had a great deal to do with his catering to middle-class taste. Clearly, if one compares Grimm's *Iron Hans* with the versions that he used, one can see that he has made the tale more sentimental, smoothed over the abrupt sequences, and propounded notions of loyalty and industriousness that were fundamental to the bourgeois ideology of his time in Germany.

Whatever the case may be, the text of *Iron Hans* is not our text, it is Grimm's but it is typical of Bly's strategy to make his appropriation appear to be a necessary reappropriation of what naturally and genuinely belongs to all men who want to be real men. Similarly his translation of the German text is also to be accepted as unquestionably authentic, but there are many dubious points in his translation which reveal how he twists the text to fit his personal conception of initiation.

For example, Bly makes and must make a great deal out of the wound that his young boy suffers. However, the word *wound* is never used in the German text, but rather the verb *schmerzen*, to hurt. The boy's finger began to hurt him terribly so that he unwillingly stuck his finger into the spring. There is no referential meaning within the text to a psychic wound in the profound manner in which Bly interprets it. If anything, the golden finger could stand for a guilty conscience that Bly never discusses—the guilt he feels for betraying his parents—or it could stand as an erect phallic symbol for the rise of puberty. Once it is hardened, there is no more pain. Significantly, this putative wound does not seem to bother our hero very much. Typically in all of the Grimms' tales the protagonists do not reflect upon their actions and interactions. Critics do. Psychologists do. And of course, poets do, so that, in the text of *Iron John*, the entire psychological dimension of the tale emanates in reality from the extraordinary imagination of Robert Bly, who stretches words into metaphors without even clarifying what liberties he is taking with the German text.

Another example, which is crucial for Bly's interpretation, is when he uses the word "invaded" to describe what occurs when the king's realm becomes a battlefield. In German the words *mit Krieg überzogen* are used, not *angegriffen* (attacked). Literally, the king's realm is overrun by war or drenched in war. But Bly wants to make it seem that, somehow the king's realm has been invaded to justify the warlike attitude of his hero as a warrior, who, Bly asserts, is called upon to defend his psyche and loved one. Yet, we do not know who started the war, how it originated, or who the enemy is. In fact, in the other Grimm version of *The Wild Man*, it is the emperor, who *attacks* England. In 1850 Wilhelm made a change. Perhaps he wanted to recall the Napoleonic Wars, when Central Europe was drenched and caught up in war. Perhaps he wanted to refer to the chaotic revolutions of 1848. But he did not state precisely that the king's realm was invaded. Bly does this, for he does not want to leave much to our imagination: *Iron John* is his text, and he wants to set the limits of our reading, as if we needed a mentor and help in reading so that we would not go astray. But as I have argued, his text and reading assume the form of a nightmare for folklorists, and his help can be more likened to the dangerous hand that Iron Hans extends from the murky pool in the forest.

But what about its nightmarish qualities for a general public? Bly's *Iron John* is a self-help book written in the tradition of the disciples of C.G. Jung and Joseph Campbell, of which he is clearly one of the chosen. The major *intended* audience of his work consists of American men who are to learn to come into contact with the wild man in them by listening to the sweet words of the lyrical wild man outside of them, who patches together strands of myths from everywhere with poetic digressions and political diatribes against industrialization, capitalism, and false American leaders. However, his words have ramifications for *all* Americans,[11] since he claims to speak in the name of men and about all men, who cannot be isolated from other human beings. The ramifications and their nightmare aspects for American progressive politics are what interest me now.

Though Bly constantly talks about overcoming the feminine side of the soft male, he purports to admire the feminist movement and pays holy tribute to goddesses and the vital energy of contemporary American women while urging men to separate themselves from these women to dig deep down in their souls and strut their own stuff. As Martin Amis has noted in his review of *Iron John*, "It hardly needs to be pointed out that Bly is phallocentric to the ends of his hair, and rollicking tendentious even in his imagery: '"The King" and "the Queen" send energy down. They resemble the sun and the moon that pierce down through the earth's atmosphere. Even on cloudy days something of their radiant energy comes through.' Yes, but the moon has no energy, and doesn't radiate; the Queen merely reflects the heavenly power of the King. Not that Bly is at all forgetful of women's interests. He wants to establish, or re-establish, a world where men are so great that women *like* being lorded over."[12] Bly's notions about men are a clear reaction to the women's movement[13] and part of a backlash against American women.[14] As Jill Johnston has incisively pointed out,

Bly, like Jung before him, is caught up in the "archetypes" of the masculine and the feminine. Men and women are defined by a given nature, fixed and unalterable, cast as opposites (the feminine embodying Eros, the masculine Logos) in a system reflecting the political status quo, under the guise of political ignorance. Bly never grasped, it seems, the core concept of feminism, that the attributes of masculinity and feminity are cultural fabrications rooted in a caste system in which one sex serves the other. You can tell he missed the point and instead imagined that feminism meant the idealization of "the feminine," the reclamation of the Great Mother, when he says, "More and more women in recent decades have begun identifying with the female pole, and main-

tain that everything bad is male, and everything good is female"
Under the influence of feminism, that was the unfortunate polar-
ization *he* made. And now, under the influence of the backlash, he
finds that "everything good" is male, or some mythic good male,
now being reclaimed.[15]

This reclamation as reaction is truly reactionary in the
fullest sense of the term, for the best that he can offer men is a
spiritual journey into themselves based on a weakly founded
atavistic thesis that "true men" in the past have found themselves with the help of the wild man. Women are reified into
archetypal figures representative of phases that a man must
pass through in order to reach a goal of self-fulfillment with a
distinct orientation to a Christlike hairy figure, who is in
touch with God and sexuality and whose advice is sought by
rulers and common people.

As I mentioned earlier, Bly makes a major distinction between the wild and the savage man, the true and the false
warrior, linking the wild man to hurricane and Zeus energy,
courage, resolve, and purity and the savage to greed, rapac-
ity, destruction, and dishonesty. Yet, he conveniently fails to
mention that the wild man, aside from having demonic
qualities both in the Grimm text and his own, is a killer. At
the beginning of *Iron Hans* and also *The Wild Man*, he kills
all the hunters who enter the forest and turns it into a place
of dread. This murderous wild man, associated with demonic forces, becomes the tutor of the king's son, just as
many aristocrats had soldiers as their tutors to harden them
like steel, and though Bly tries to rationalize the young
man's militaristic drives later on as belonging to self-defense, it is clear that the young hero at the end of the tale
has sought to impress his future father-in-law and wife with
his prowess as a fighter and killer. The young man likes to
strut his stuff, and he is certainly encouraged to do so both
by Iron Hans and the king, who knows how to bring out his
aggressive and competitive urges by holding a tournament.

And the young man will stop at nothing to win, to impress the king and his daughter, and obviously to win the daughter as prize: the princess views herself and is made into a prize and takes a secondary role to the golden-haired boy, who shines his light on her.

Both *Iron Hans* and *Iron John* are *warrior* tales, and both celebrate violence and killing as the means to establish male identity. In the case of Bly's narrative, it sadly rationalizes the militaristic tendencies of American culture that were manifested during the Persian Gulf War. As Sharon Doubiago stated, "the use of 'devotional' books to inspire warrior energy is an ancient one. For me, in Paris, a city warrior-crazed like the rest of the world, the Shadow of Robert Bly stepped forward to join those of George Bush and Saddam Hussein, a trinity fusing into the mythic figure of Goliath massacring David—to the score of 100,000 to 148. Ever since, of course, in the same kind of blatant lie that permits Bly to insist that his book is not antifemale, he's maintained that the Gulf War was *perverted* warrior energy. But using his own archetypal ideology, *there are no coincidences. Iron John* is our Desert Storm book." [16]

What is really new about *Iron John*'s notions of sex roles and war? Why has Bly turned *Iron Hans* and twisted it every which way and milked it to produce his contemporary myth of male initiation? As I have suggested, the journey in this book is Bly's story, a personal odyssey, and in a remarkably compassionate reading of this book, Ted Solotaroff has traced the parallels between Bly's interpretation of the *Iron Hans* story to Bly's personal development: "Like most literary careers that last, Bly's has been formed from the ongoing play of oppositions, but his have been particularly intense: Lutheran and pagan, rural and international, reclusive and engaged, austere and grandiose. These contending traits and inclinations have generated Bly's high energy and also created a certain rhythm to his career that makes his present celebrity and function almost predictable.

Also they are compacted into a strongly lived life that per-
sonalizes the mythopoetic structure and far-out counsel of
Iron John and gives the book, for all of its discursiveness
and highhandedness, an overall staying power and a kind of
charmed ability to hit paydirt about every third page." [17]
The difficulty is that Bly intends "his story" to be *history*, to
be more than his story and to help change men's lives. For
Solotaroff, Bly manages to hit paydirt, whatever that may
mean, in "soul-making" every few pages, but clearly the
ideological message and confused notions of his book con-
tradict his own progressive politics.

As is well known, Bly has had a remarkable career as an
antiwar activist and inspirational leader for a large segment
of the men's movement in the United States. [18] In a recent
interview with Kim Ode, he stated:

The reason we have a men's movement now is that sons have been
separated from their fathers for three or four generations in an
increasingly severe way. There is a tremendous mourning and sons
have what could be called father hunger. . . . what I've seen happen to the men will probably happen to the daughters also, and
it's being forced by capitalism. It's being forced by international
industrialization. . . . What international industrialization is doing is slash-and-burn, the way we treat a forest. We don't wait for
a full-growth forest, which would mean taking care of the children and seeing that they are well-rounded. We practice slash-
and-burn culture instead. We use up the parents and you get these
abandoned-looking children you see in malls. And international
industrialization doesn't care. If we can take profits off the top,
we'll do it, and we don't intend to think of what life will be like
20 years from now, 40 years from now. [19]

This statement is right on the mark, and every now and
then in *Iron John* there are remarks like this, but the overall
tendentious argument of Bly's book distracts the reader
from capitalism and international industrialization to induce the male reader to think that he can heal his wound,
the separation from the father, by undergoing a spiritual

quest for his wildness. Moreover, Bly is obsessed by this one wound, as though separation from the father were *the* wound common to *all* men.

But where in his treatise are all the wounds that men cause? There is no discussion of the manifold disturbances in family and personal life caused by the development of capitalism; no class, gender, or racial distinctions made in Bly's diagnosis of the malaise affecting men; no consideration of the economic factors of unemployment and bureaucratization that cause violence in and outside the family; no consideration of why men have become more soft and violent at the same time, leaving women more victimized since the 1970s than ever before. Instead, Bly seeks to homogenize man through the use of archetypes developed by Jung and Campbell, whose theories about myths and collective unconscious overlook the specificity of real types of human beings, blur the dynamic interaction between sociogenetic and psychogenetic forces in the civilizing process, and encourage nostalgic longings for atavistic models of the past that never existed in the first place. By universalizing the malaise of the American male so that it can be understood on a level of the mythopoetic, Bly defeats his own political purpose and undermines the cause of many political thinkers who are rigorously analyzing our culture from a multicultural perspective and trying to differentiate with respect to the needs of very different people. In addition, Bly goes against many thinkers in both the men's and women's movements who have been trying to come to terms with gender and sexuality as social constructs. There is a pronounced proclivity in Bly's thinking to view gender formation as an organic and eternal process that can only be grasped in myth.

In his brilliant analysis of contemporary mythmaking, the French semiotician Roland Barthes remarked,

myth is constituted by the loss of the historical quality of things: in it, things lose the memory that they once were made. The world

enters language as a dialectical relation between activities, between human actions; it comes out of myth as a harmonious display of essences. A conjuring trick has taken place; it has turned
reality inside out, it has emptied it of history and has filled it with
nature, it has removed from things their human meaning so as to
make them signify a human insignificance. The function of myth
is to empty reality; it is, literally, a ceaseless flowing out, a haem-
orrhage, or perhaps an evaporation, in short a perceptible ab-
sence. . . . *myth is depoliticized speech.*[20]

Robert Bly's *Iron John* is American myth in its most
powerful depoliticized form. The "bucketing-out process"
that he prescribes for American men at the beginning of his
book is ironically nothing but the means to empty readers'
minds so that they will be receptive to poetical notions of
male hegemony and of harmony between essential mythical
archetypes that conceal the unique nature of people in history. The nightmare and hyperbole in Bly's spreading myths
about the fairy tale of *Iron Hans* should make readers think
twice before they follow Bly's path of initiation.

5. OZ AS AMERICAN MYTH

Utopian novels are written in the indicative about the political subjunctive. They treat contemporary political and social conditions and raise questions about how they might or should be changed. Whether conservative or progressive, the narrative strategies of different authors intend to distance us from our present world so that we can explore change. Paradoxically, they remove us from our present situation to engage us with it. Their futuristic or otherworldly settings are deceiving, for they only set the framework for the author's political critique of the here and now, inviting readers to share the deception and confront the critique. It is within deception that the truth lies. It is within fantasy that the political unconscious can awaken and map out the space which it needs and had been denied. L. Frank Baum knew this intuitively when he first wrote *The Wonderful Wizard of Oz*. However, he did not realize that his imagination was to become the funnel for a national political unconscious. Oz is everything America did not become, and it is why we keep trying to return to Oz.

But returning to Oz is not going backward. It is a leap forward, a flight forward, a utopian gesture. It is our endeavor to recapture promises of the past and fulfill them by making our mark in the present. Oz is a marker. It sets apart the utopian imagination from the cynical. It is the measure of hope, a secular force of humanitarian hope.

Illustration by
W. W. Denslow, 1900.

Illustration by
W. W. Denslow, 1900.

It is fascinating to see how Oz took on its force and captured the national imagination in America. As we know, Baum was an Easterner who traveled and experienced the Midwest during the 1890s, a period of upheaval, depression, and crisis. Settled, but really unsettled in Chicago, Baum, the wanderer, conceived the first narrative of Oz at a time when the American frontier had just closed. There was no more space to conquer in America, and whatever manifest destiny may have been, Baum had seen its spoiled fruits in the Midwest. Oz was what Kansas was not, what Nebraska, North Dakota, South Dakota, and Illinois were not. It was the ungray place where a young girl could come into contact with the qualities she would need (courage, brains, and heart) and realize her potential through nonviolent means in opposition to conmen and wicked witches. Only after a visit to Oz could Dorothy take on Kansas. Not accept Kansas, but take on Kansas to change it. Just as Baum himself sought to realize his dreams and visions in the Midwest and later the West.

As we know, however, Baum failed, and America failed Baum. That is, Baum failed in numerous business enterprises, but he never really failed as a writer. He became the chronicler of America's failure, and in his series of fourteen Oz books, he depicted how Dorothy was gradually compelled to leave America forever and settle in Oz. The conmen, bankers, and cynical people envelop America, fix its boundaries, and as Baum died in 1919, the Wobblie movement was about to be annihilated in America. A new world order was coming into being. It was not communism, but the beginnings of a Cold War, the division of the world into good and evil zones, the so-called free world and the world of dictators. Binary thinking was celebrated. There were to be no in-betweens. And yet, there were many in-betweens, cracks in the settlement of the forty-eight states, fissures, places where one could still glimpse Oz, escape to Oz, and return to America with recharged hope.

So it was not by chance that various writers continued to write Oz books after Baum's death, and it was especially not coincidental that, during the years of the Depression, the cinematic version of *The Wonderful Wizard of Oz* was conceived and completed by 1939 with many of its co-creators associated with socialist and left-wing causes.[1] Oz was resurrected out of the misery of the 1930s, an alternate vision of America, a mirror that reflected America's disgrace and promise. Somewhere over the rainbow there was a land we all dream of, and ironically it was realized through the cooperative efforts of numerous people and marked as fantasy. But, in fact, the fantasy was the real, materialist outcome of the needs of individuals who in a group effort wanted to mark what was missing in American society.

Oz as a hopeful measure of lack in America. The film did not have an immediate impact as political critique. That is, it was a success, but a moderate success. It had to wait for 1956 before it became a national success and political monument of our failure and hope. Interestingly, it was disseminated through TV and had a powerful effect as cinematic fantasy during the 1950s, stamped by the McCarthy inquisitions, the Rosenberg trial, and the Korean War. Then as now, Oz was what America was not. Oz as national iconic representation was truth denied, reality unfulfilled. Both film and book formed a utopian constellation, a reference point by the beginning of the 1960s, one that fortunately has not gone away and compels us to return time and again to determine our national character and identity.

Of course, one may take issue with my short narrative of how Oz came into being as an American myth, that is, how it has not come into being or been fulfilled in reality. As utopian icon, Oz has stood and stands for many things, and it is always important to clarify as much as one can what Oz is as reference point: Is it the Oz of Baum's first book, *The Wonderful Wizard of Oz*? Is it the sum of all fourteen books? Is it the Oz of the MGM film of 1939? Is it a mix of the MGM

film and Baum's books? Do we associate it with escape? Is it
subversive and harmful to children as some librarians asserted during the 1950s? What is the difference between Peter
Pan's never-never land and Dorothy's Oz? Is there really
something peculiarly American about Oz? What do politics
have to do with the fanciful land of Oz?

To answer these questions, one would have to write a reception history of Oz as myth and icon, something that Paul
Nathanson has meticulously tried to do in his book *Over the
Rainbow: The Wizard of Oz as a Secular Myth of America*.[2]
Though Nathanson is primarily concerned with the film adaptation of Baum's fairy-tale novel, he does see both as constituting the rise of an American secular myth that is a prototypical sacred story concerned with an initiation process that
most Americans share. On an individual level, Dorothy, as the
"American" protagonist, learns to gather together basic ar-
chetypical attributes represented by the scarecrow, the tin
woodsman, and the cowardly lion in exile. Using a Jungian
methodology, Nathanson shows how she assembles these archetypes harmoniously within her psyche by the end of her
adventures and thus can return to make a contribution to her
community. On a societal level, Dorothy's experiences have
more to do with the American collective unconscious, and
here Nathanson reads the film as containing elements of
myth and religion, for the MGM *Wizard of Oz* is allegedly
about the fall from grace and the quest for redemption. Banished from Kansas as paradise, Nathanson maintains, Dorothy wants to return to this tranquil garden:

Kansas is not immediately revealed as paradise. The movie begins
(in the prologue) not with Dorothy's "prelapsarian" life in Kansas
but with her "fall" and "expulsion." This is because Kansas is
always seen through Dorothy's eyes; if she is unable to "see" truly
in the prologue she is able to do so after returning from Oz in the
epilogue. Consequently, Kansas is not only the end of the movie, it
is also the End. It is the world as it will be at the *eschaton*. In the
prologue, Dorothy is forced by a serpentine tornado to leave

home. Otherwise, she could not have reached the level of maturity necessary to understand the meaning of being at home with her family, being at home in the world at large and (by implication) being at home with God. In the epilogue, she is ready to take her proper place at home in the world and (by implication) with God. The main difference is to be found not in Kansas but in Dorothy herself. In the epilogue, unlike the prologue, she has "eyes to see and ears to hear."

Ultimately, then, *The Wizard* is a statement of faith not only in the individual and the nation but in the cosmic matrix of both. Despite the perils, despite the lapses into chaos, life in this world is worth living because there is an underlying order that can be experienced partly now (in everyday life) and fully then (in another life beyond the flux of time and space). And what was true of America in 1939 is true also of America today.[3]

For Nathanson, the film version that continually re-enters our homes through television in the form of a secular ritual also expresses a certain iconic ambiguity that makes it especially appealing to Americans. Instead of rejecting Oz—which Nathanson insists represents high technology, modernity, and progress—in favor of the pastoral paradise of Kansas—symbolizing the frontier, agriculture, low technology, tradition, and stasis—the film maintains the tension between the two. As he states, "What is distinctive about *The Wizard* is that instead of affirming one and condemning the other, it affirms both. It does not present a radical statement, to be sure, but it does not present a reactionary one either. It was (and may still be) necessary for Americans to hold these two perspectives in tension. If the enduring popularity of *The Wizard* is taken seriously, this ambiguous solution has been a very successful response to the problem of collective identity in a rapidly changing world."

Perhaps, if one believes in such a thing as collective identity and the collective unconscious. Both these categories are not only difficult to define, but they are also questionable as valid tools for comprehending mass reception and individual psychology. Is there such a thing as an American collective identity or American collective unconscious? Doesn't the notion of what American means keep changing? Is Kansas symbolic of an American paradise? Does Dorothy undergo an American initiation ritual that will make her happy and secure in Kansas? Is Dorothy's gender-specific experience and development a prototypical secular religious experience with which most Americans relate and which most Americans desire? Nathanson cannot satisfactorily answer these questions because the categories that he takes from Jung and Mircea Eliade are forced upon the film, leading to a fundamental misinterpretation of the film and the mythic power of the icon Oz itself.

First of all, to posit Kansas as some kind of paradise to which Dorothy wishes to return is a distortion of the beginning of the film. We must remember that the black and white monochrome beginning and end must be contrasted to the technicolor of the Oz dream sequence. In other words, just as Baum painted Kansas as drab and gray, so did the creators of the film version. Of course, they also softened Baum's image by making the farm and surroundings less hostile and forbidding. Nevertheless, the environment cannot be equated with a paradise. Dorothy feels threatened. Miss Gulch, the richest woman in the country, is about to exterminate Dorothy's dog Toto, and Aunt Em and Uncle Henry cannot stop her. There is, in fact, no resistance to the tyrant, who has the law on her side. The picture that we have of Kansas and farm life in the prologue has nothing to do with a pastoral paradise. Aunt Em and Uncle Henry have introduced incubators into the farm, and it is obvious that they are receptive to the age of mechanization. They are so consumed by their work that Dorothy is ignored and told to keep out of trouble. All this leads her to sing her famous song;

Somewhere, over the rainbow, way up high,
There's a land that I heard of once in a lullaby.
Somewhere, over the rainbow, skies are blue,

And the dreams that you dare to dream really do
  come true.

Someday I'll wish upon a star
And wake up where the clouds are far behind me,
Where troubles melt like lemon drops,
Away above the chimney tops
That's where you'll find me.

Somewhere over the rainbow, bluebirds fly,
Birds fly over the rainbow,
Why then, oh why can't I?[4]

It is clear from her original distressed situation and this
song that Dorothy *desires* to leave Kansas, where she is
bored, neglected, and threatened. If there is a paradise, it is
conceived out of her utopian longing and it is way beyond
Kansas. It is something that Dorothy realizes that she must
find or create, and she runs away from home to do this. The
only reason she returns in the film is because Professor
Marvel shames her into feeling sorry about Aunt Em. This
emotional blackmail sends Dorothy back to the farm where
she is knocked unconscious by the cyclone hitting the house.

Unlike Baum's novel, in which Dorothy is actually carried
to a real place named Oz, the film depicts Dorothy dreaming
of her experiences in Oz. To a certain extent, this dream is
unnecessary because Dorothy had already found the courage
and heart to return home to face the circumstances of the
tumultuous farm life in Kansas. Therefore, the dream concerns her fear and guilt of losing home and also reconfirms
the self-confidence that she has also demonstrated. Dorothy
has always had it in her through the ruby/silver shoes to go
home whenever she wished.

When she does make it home, (that is, when she wakes
up) nothing has changed in Kansas. Her dream of Oz is not
taken seriously by her aunt and uncle and the farmhands
because they know reality and are simply glad that Dorothy
has survived. They are all survivors, and Dorothy is glad to

be home. Though she asserts that "there's no place like home,"[5] she is more reconciled to home because of her experiences in the utopia of Oz.

Neither the film nor the novel, as Nathanson suggests, celebrates America as home. On the contrary, it is Oz as symbol of wish-fulfillment dreams, as the symbolical embodiment of the longing for a better life, as the utopian realm in which justice is attained that is the key icon of the film and novel. Dorothy cannot rid Kansas of rich tyrants like Miss Gulch and the bankers who hold the mortgage to the farm of Uncle Henry and Aunt Em. Kansas will remain stark, and Dorothy must and does face up to this fact because she wants the love of Aunt Em and Uncle Henry and needs their recognition. However, only through experiencing the strange utopia of Oz, learning about aliens and other ways, does Kansas become bearable.

Nathanson argues that Kansas is home as paradise. However, as the philosopher Ernst Bloch has revealed in his remarkable opus, *The Principle of Hope*, home is not a place we actually know or have known. We are constantly creating home out of our longings, desires, and dreams. As Bloch has stated, "*The true genesis is not at the beginning, but at the end*, and it starts to begin only when society and existence become radical; that is, comprehend their own roots. But the root of history is the working, creating man, who rebuilds and transforms the given circumstances of the world. Once man has comprehended himself and has established his own domain in real democracy, without depersonalization and alienation, something arises in the world which all men have glimpsed in childhood: a place and a state in which no one has yet been. And the name of this something is home or homeland."[6]

Philosophically speaking, the return home is a move forward to what has been repressed and never fulfilled. The pattern in most fairy tales—and *The Wizard of Oz* is a fairy tale as novel and film—involves the reconstitution of home on a new plane, and this accounts for the power of its appeal to both children and adults. Phrased another way, if there is a mythic appeal in *The Wizard of Oz* as film and novel to Americans, it is owing to the glimpse that we all receive of a utopian counterpart to America, what America could become but has not.

Baum himself sensed the failure of the promise of America to become paradise, and this is the reason that he kept sending Dorothy back to Oz over the course of fourteen novels and eventually had her remain (with Aunt Em and Uncle Henry) in Oz, safe from the capitalist bankers and Eastern businessmen in America. And, throughout the past century, Americans keep returning to the Oz material not because of the American myth but because of the promises that America as a nation has failed to keep. Oz is the utopia that exposes the myth of America as land of the free and brave as lie.

The political implications of Oz as utopia have not always been realized in the adaptations of the various Oz books nor are they explicit in our veneration of Baum's Oz materials. But the significance in the particular way Americans have received and worked with Baum's utopian vision of Oz is connected to the gaps that we feel in our lives, to political and social deprivation that keeps us wishing for home in Oz.

Two recent utopian revisions of Baum's Oz demonstrate how we use a return to Oz to project alternate worlds and possibilities to the America that we experience in the present. As case studies I shall analyze Philip José Farmer's *A Barnstormer in Oz* (1982) and Geoff Ryman's *Was* (1992), emphasizing re-vision as re-viewing, that is, looking again at Baum's Oz and the MGM Oz. Both Farmer and Ryman are thoroughly familiar with the Oz novels and the film, and they both critically review the Oz material to recast it in a different mold. Interestingly, these two splended works were conceived during a reactionary trend in the United

States, against the material and cultural impoverishment caused by the Reagan and Bush governments, and therefore signal hope in desperate years, just as the original book and film did at the turn of the century and during the 1930s. Whether the signal will have an impact and produce new insights about the necessity for change depends on how Oz is re-constructed in a particular novel and received by readers. Therefore, I am primarily interested in the narrative constructs of Farmer and Ryman, for it is through their artistic constructs that their political critiques best can be carried home. And home is what Oz is all about.

Farmer's narrative strategy in *A Barnstormer in Oz* is ingenious in this respect, for Hank Stover, a twenty-year-old pilot, finds home in Oz when he least expects it. Nor does it seem that he will abandon it. On April 1, 1923, Hank stumbles upon Oz while he is flying his Jenny over Kansas. He pierces a mysterious green cloud and is surprised to find himself in Oz. What is even more surprising for readers, after Glinda the good witch meets Hank, is the discovery that Hank is actually Dorothy's son (Dorothy is still alive and married to a wealthy New Englander, son of a stockbroker) and that Baum had not told the entire truth about Dorothy's history. Once this initial situation is fabricated, Farmer can now begin playing with a range of possibilities that will enable him to enhance the utopian potential of Oz (with humor, or course) and elaborate a political critique of the American "world order" of the early 1980s.

Told by a third-person omniscient narrator, whom we can assume to be Farmer, because he provides us with author's notes at the end of the novel, we are led to believe that this seemingly fictitious story about certain events in 1923 is really true and contradicts many things that Baum had previously told us about Dorothy and Oz. For instance, when Glinda wants to know what had happened to Dorothy after leaving Oz, we are informed that she returned not to Kansas but to Aberdeen, South Dakota, her actual hometown, where

Baum, who recorded her story, was a journalist. As Stover tells Glinda,

What I have to explain is that an Earthman, and American, wrote a book about Dorothy's adventures here. . . . But it was fiction or purported to be. Actually, much of it was fiction. And the parts that were true were bowdlerized. They had to be because he was writing a book for children. . . . Mother was gone for six months, but, in the book this man, Lyman Frank Baum, wrote about her, she was here for only a few weeks. This man Baum was a fiction writer but at the time was the editor of a newspaper in Aberdeen. He heard about the little girl whom everybody thought had been carried off by the tornado. Her body was searched for but not found. People thought that she'd probably been dropped into a ravine or woods many miles from Aberdeen. Maybe the coyotes had eaten her. Then my mother showed up with a tale of having been transported to some unknown land beyond the desert in Arizona Territory.[7]

Based on a series of three interviews, we learn from Stover, Baum thought that Dorothy had probably suffered from delirium after surviving a tornado and later published *The Wonderful Wizard of Oz* as pure fiction. Therefore, it is Baum's fiction that actually needs to be revised in a fictional work that purports to be fact and a "true" account of the real Dorothy's son in the real Oz. The narrative game is obvious, and Farmer wryly plays with the reader's familiarity with Oz material and expectations to send Stover on a mission that recalls Dorothy's initial adventures in Oz. This time, however, the mission is more complicated, for Oz is threatened from outside as well as within.

Apparently, Stover's plane slipped through an opening in the green cloud because of secret experiments undertaken by the Signal Corps at Fort Leavenworth, and he was spotted by surveillance. Consequently, the American military wants to make use of him so that it can set up a base in Oz and eventually colonize it. At the same time, a wicked red witch named Erakna has taken over the land of the Gillikins and uses her powerful forces, including the winged monkeys, to try to overthrow Glinda. Hank, who has an amorous affair with a pert Quadling named Lamblo, and who admires the tantalizing Glinda, becomes more and more captivated by the social life of Oz and committed to saving it from the American military and the tyrannical Erakna. Here it should be stated that Oz is not the perfect utopian world that Baum described. Yet, as Hank experiences it under Glinda's benevolent dictatorship, it is a society in which everything is alive, talks, and is respected. The people are vegetarian; the animals have equal rights and are sentient, as are many objects, including Hank's plane Jenny. Murder and rape are punished by expulsion or death. There is birth control, and men are the ones who are responsible for taking contraception drinks. Guns and other types of automatic weapons are not permitted. Though not a matriarchal society, Oz is certainly influenced by social and moral principles generally associated with women, and consequently, the people are kind and gentle except when aroused.

Nevertheless, it is not easy for Hank to adopt Oz as his home, for he feels manipulated by the mysterious Glinda, and he is constantly tested by her to see whether he would indeed fit into the Ozian mold. Eventually, Hank is forced to declare his allegiance when a squadron of American soldiers are sent to establish an outpost in Oz and to prepare for an eventual colonization that is based on greed for the precious stones in Oz. Since Hank does not want to be a traitor to his country, he goes to the American camp and warns the captain that he and his men are being used.

"This land is lousy with rubies, diamonds, emeralds—up north is a whole city studded with emeralds—topazes, turquoises, tourmalines. And there's gold, Captain, more gold than in a thousand Klondikes and a hundred South Africas. And there's silver enough to build the Great Wall of China.

"I tell you, Captain, the men who get their hands on this

wealth will be super-Croesuses. But they'll have to keep tight control on it. Otherwise, earth'll be flooded with precious stones and
metals, the bottom would drop out of the market, and earth
would be in financial chaos.

"So, it's greed that's behind this. The big shots who sent you
here to die don't care about you. If you're wiped out, they'll have
a good excuse to send in more poor devils to fight and die for
them. For the wealth they want. I wouldn't put it past them to
send in men suffering from smallpox and cholera and all the sick-
nesses in Pandora's box. They'd spread their diseases, and just
about everybody in this world would die."[8]

But before that can happen, Glinda and her forces attack
the American soldiers and wipe them out. Hank is saddened
by this act, but he realizes Glinda had no choice, and he
continues to help her when she makes a secret visit to the
dying President Harding in San Francisco and plants a sign
that will prevent the Americans from making any more attempts at invading Oz. After that daring flight to America,
Glinda summons up all her powers to vanquish Erakna, and
Hank lives on in Oz, awed by Glinda's magnificent goodness.

There is more to this novel than my brief synopsis of the
narrative construct reveals. There is Farmer's introduction
of fabulous characters including new descriptions of the Tin
Woodman, the Scarecrow, and the Cowardly Lion. There is
also his ironic commentary on the Oz books and vivid depiction of battle and action scenes. Yet, most important is
his insistence on pursuing the utopian project of Oz that
transforms home into a critique of American imperialism
and celebrates tolerance for other lifestyles. His optimism is
catching, and in this regard makes him a faithful heir of the
Baum tradition, despite his poking fun at L. Frank. In fact,
it is Farmer's hilarious style that makes his political critique
so effective.

It is not 1923, nor is it the American military industrial
complex of the 1920s that Farmer rejects. Rather, he moves
into the past to recall the American military adventures in

Illustration by W.W. Denslow, 1900.

South Vietnam, South America, and elsewhere during the 1970s and 1980s. He raises the issue of birth and weapon control, ecological preservation, and animal rights to map the possibilities for American society in the near future. Rarely does Farmer preach to make his point. Instead, it is by showing in his narrative where Baum made up a fictitious account, where he went wrong, that we can go right and do good. Undermining Baum, he actually remains loyal to him, and in this sense he too acts as a funnel for the American imagination and questions what it means to break one's allegiance to one's country and to be an American.

National identity is not so important to Geoff Ryman in his revision of Oz in his novel *Was*, nor is humor. Ryman is much more somber than Farmer, and yet his project is similar insofar as he wants to correct Baum's vision and reveal the truth in Baum's deceptive fantasy and consequently make an appeal for the realistic implications of the utopian vision.

Ryman frames his narrative by beginning with a chapter that takes place in Manhattan, Kansas, September 1989, and ending with a chapter set in Rose Lawn Farm, near Syracuse, New York, during the summer of 1861. In the first chapter, Jonathan, an actor, who had played the Scarecrow in a stage production of *The Wonderful Wizard of Oz* in California, is dying of AIDS and is seeking the origins of the Oz story to come to terms with his own destiny. In the closing chapter, Jonathan has disappeared after fulfilling his quest, and we are returned to L. Frank Baum's childhood in Rose Lawn Farm, where Frank has hidden from his nanny because he doesn't like her. When his mother finds him, she explains to Frank that the nanny doesn't always understand, that she doesn't always remember what it is like to be a child. The novel then closes with Frank promising, "I'll remember."[9]

Remembering childhood, what Oz really was, is the major concern of Ryman's revision of *The Wonderful Wizard of Oz*. Essentially it is the remembering of three childhoods: Dorothy's, Judy Garland's, and Jonathan's. And Ryman skillfully weaves their lives together in episodes that span a century of American history in such a vivid manner that the differences between fantasy and reality evaporate. What becomes concretely significant is the political unconscious of childhood and recalling the repressed, which means rewriting the "true' history of Dorothy Gael with all its ramifications, for Baum had only caught a glimpse of the sordid gray conditions of Kansas when, according to Ryman, he had been an itinerant actor substituting as teacher at a small town school in Kansas.

Rewriting history takes on a fantastic textual form in Ryman's novel with lives linked in episodic time leaps back and forth unraveling the mystery of Dorothy's destiny in what was not the "utopian" Oz (as Baum portrayed it) and yet was Oz in reality. The confusion of what Oz was takes the form of a mystery, and compelled to read as detectives, we follow the clues of Dorothy's odyssey *not* down the Yellow Brick Road, but down barren dirt roads that eventually lead to a sterile old-age home in Zeandale. But before this we learn that Dorothy Gael had been sent to Zeandale, a small town outside Manhattan, Kansas, in 1875 after her mother and brother had died from diphtheria in St. Louis. Her mother had earlier run away with an actor to escape Kansas, but he had abandoned her some time before her death. Now, Dorothy has to face what her mother had tried to avoid: life in a small town with her mother's pious frustrated sister, Aunt Em, and her grubby husband, Uncle Henry Gulch. Upon welcoming her, these two "well-meaning" grown-ups proceed to cut her hair and destroy her clothes to get the disease out of her, and soon after they kill her pesky dog Toto because he cannot be tamed, Dorothy grows up only to be raped and violated by Uncle Henry, despised by the schoolchildren in Manhattan, and driven to prostitution in Wichita. She ends her days in a state nursing home, safely at home in her madness, but a threat to the wardens or anyone who tries to come too close to the world that she has built for herself.

Though Judy Garland's childhood was not ruined by physical abuse, she did suffer from a mother who exploited her and took out her frustrations on her family. If Judy becomes hard, mendacious, and difficult as an adolescent only to commit suicide as an adult, it is, as Ryman suggests, because she was tortured as a gifted child and made to feel responsible for the fortunes of her family.

Jonathan, who had grown up somewhat autistic in a small town in Canada, saw *The Wonderful Wizard of Oz*, starring Judy Garland in 1956, and it was the Oz story that enabled him to come out of himself and eventually use his talents to become an actor in California. At one point, after he had become famous by starring in horror films, Jonathan was drawn to play the scarecrow in the dramatic adaptation of the novel, and he sensed with the guidance of his psychiatrist, Bill, who just happened to know old Dorothy Gael, when he was an aid in the nursing home in Kansas, that tracing the history of the origins of Oz might help him come to terms with his disease and death.

Symbolically, it is over and through Jonathan's diseased body that Ryman conceives his political critique of American society. It is not Jonathan who is diseased, not Dorothy who was crazy, nor Judy Garland who was suicidal. They are all rather indices in a reconstructed narrative of an Oz that was, and as indices they point to murderous rites of upbringing in America that cause the destruction of some of our most talented and imaginative children. Strongly influenced by the Swiss psychiatrist Alice Miller, whose works he cites during the course of his highly complex narrative, Ryman is preoccupied with showing how children are constantly at the mercy of adults and suffer psychological and physical abuse even though parents may want the best for their children. In Dorothy's case, it is the provinciality, religious narrowness, and arbitrary violence of midwestern towns, and in Judy Garland's case it is the desire for material success and sexual frustration of her mother, that drive them to flee home in search of Oz, a real home. Only Jonathan, who is Canadian, appears to have had understanding parents and escaped the small-town provincialism in Canada with minor damage caused by his peers, who bullied him. And it is Jonathan, who carries the hope for the future.

Though faced with death, Jonathan wants to remember, to remember Dorothy, Judy Garland, the towns of Zeandale and Manhattan, the farm where Dorothy was raped, and the schoolhouse where L. Frank Baum taught. Johnathan wants to remember and write against rape and violation, customary practices in the contemporary land of the free. By recalling the repressed history of America, Ryman urgently compels readers to recall why we have arrived at the present. Was (Oz) was not a fictitious place, but very real, and Ryman calls upon us to turn the nightmare reality into what Baum's Oz was, that is, a gentle utopia, where neither human beings nor animals are ravaged, but where relations are determined through the fostering of self-esteem and love.

In the afterword entitled "Reality Check" at the end of Was, Ryman states,

Oz is, after all, only a place with flowers and birds, and rivers and hills. Everything is alive there, as it is here if we care to see it. Tomorrow, we could all decide to live in a place not much different from Oz. We don't. We continue to make the world an ugly, even murderous place, for reasons we do not understand.

Those reasons lie in both fantasy and history. Where we are gripped by history—our own personal history, our country's history. Where we are deluded by fantasy, our country's fantasy. It is necessary to distinguish between history and fantasy wherever possible.

And then use them against each other.[10]

It is by using fantasy and history against each other that Ryman and Farmer, too, are able to create highly significant political critiques of America in their utopian novels and, in fact, to present reasons that we continue to make the world a murderous place. Though their works are extremely different in style, mood, and structure, Farmer and Ryman devise similar narrative strategies to revise our notions of the Oz material. Their plot is to send their protagonists out of this world, namely out of America, never to return. That is, they return to Oz but go forward in history and with a utopian gesture that will enable us as readers to follow if we care and dare.

Oz is not just any utopia. It is a specific American utopia, which may appear to be a contradiction in terms, for a utopia is no place. But Oz *is* a place and space in the American imagination, and as such it embodies that which is missing, lacking, absent in America. Oz is the counterpart to the reality of America, a possibility that has never been realized except in the imagination of writers such as Baum and his heirs. It is in constant need of revision, review, and reconstruction because social and material conditions in America keep changing. Unfortunately, these conditions have deteriorated to such an extent that Dorothy's son, a daredevil skilled pilot, and Jonathan, an aficionado of Baum and talented actor, take flight from America. They recognize what has caused disease and death in America and refuse to be implicated in the crimes. However, their flight is not an escape but a refusal, just as the narrative reconstructions of Oz by Farmer and Ryman are also refusals and simultaneously stories filled with hope to *engage* us in a critical review of our present world order.

Somewhere, Hank Stover still lives. Somewhere Jonathan is still alive and fighting his disease. That somewhere is Oz, and it is still not out of our reach.

6. THE CONTEMPORARY AMERICAN FAIRY TALE

You can always tell when Christmas is approaching in America. Sometime in November the bookstores begin displaying glossy fairy-tale books with attractive colors and startling designs in their windows. It is almost like magic, and the store windows appear to be enchanted by these marvelous books. Of course, there is really nothing magical about this phenomenon. It is absolutely predictable: storeowners and publishers are in collusion, seeking to entice both children and parents to buy as many books as possible during the holiday season. In most cases, it does not matter if the contents of the books are vapid. It is the fluff that counts, the ornament, the diverting cover designs that promise a wonderful world of pleasure and take the onlooker away from the harsh realities of the present. In the bookstore window there is the glow of difference and the promise of pleasure. In the fairy-tale books there is hope for a world distinctly more exciting and rewarding than the everyday world in the here and now.

But is there any basis for such hope? Are the fairy tales in America mere commodities that compensate for the technological evolution that has narrowed the range of possibilities for developing the imagination and humane relationships in reality? What socio-cultural function do fairy tales have in an American society, in which the most ex-

treme fantasies *and* nightmares have been coolly and brutal-
ly realized so that little is left for the imagination?

In a significant study of the historical development of the
literary fairy tale, Friedmar Apel has argued that, from its
origins, the central theme of the fairy tale has always concerned the struggle of the imagination (representing the
spiritual side of humanity) against the hard reality of exploitation and reification (representing the rise of inhumane
technology). Whereas the earlier fairy tales of the eighteenth and nineteenth centuries could optimistically project
a harmony of soul and reality brought about by magic or a
fantastic element that seemed commensurate with progress
in the world, Apel has claimed that the modern temper is
stamped by our conscious recognition that such harmony
can never be achieved and thus the very basis of the fairy
tale is no longer relevant and can never again be valid, unless its formal characteristics totally change. As he states:

While other genres (i.e., the novel, lyric poetry) have been able to
maintain themselves only by depicting the impossibility of the
unity of the world and soul, the fairy tale requires the possibility
of conceptualizing this unity as a starting point, no matter how
relativized it becomes. Without this possibility, the fairy tale must
give up its formal function of depicting the marvelous (das Wun-
derbare), unless it wants to degenerate into mere entertainment
literature by feigning harmony and thus losing all connection to
actual life. . . . all new endeavors to portray the marvelous with
the traditional means of the fairy tale and other fantastic stories
only serve to amuse the imagination and can no longer fulfill the
old functions of conveying a sublime interpretation of life and a
way of putting the meaning into practice.[1]

In short, Apel dismisses the profound utopian value,
which the fairy tale, either as oral or literary product, once
had, and he asserts that it is impossible in the twentieth
century for it to be anything more than *divertissement*, escape literature, a cultural commodity that is part of the en-

tertainment business. His position is obviously a radical one and must be qualified, if we are to understand the development and the present function of the literary fairy tale in the West, and more specifically in America. Certainly, if we look at the Walt Disney industry and the vast distribution of bowdlerized and sanitized versions of fairy tales by Perrault, the Grimms, Bechstein, Collodi, and other classical authors, it is apparent that they have been incorporated into the western culture industry mainly to amuse children and adults alike.

Yet, amusement is not to be taken lightly, for distraction and divertissement have an important ideological function: almost all the major classical fairy tales that have achieved prominence and are to be enjoyed in the United States can be considered as products that reinforce a patriarchal and middle-class social code. Their meaning is not limited to this ideological function. For instance, even if their purpose is to amuse and pacify the rebellious instincts of readers, they are received by the public in different and unpredictable ways. Although a text may contain directives within it, it cannot prescribe its effect. Meaning shifts with the individual in history. And, if the more serious fairy tales of the twentieth century and specifically contemporary American fairy tales are to have any meaning today, then we must begin at first in the production phase with the proposition that many authors believe that the classical works are indeed patriarchal and anachronistic and have served an ideological function that needs to be replaced, or, at the very least, to be revised in light of the major socio-political changes since World War II.

Bearing this in mind, the literary fairy tale of the twentieth century, despite what Apel asserts, has maintained a crucial utopian function when it is self-reflective and experimental. By questioning the forms and themes that the fairy tale has traditionally developed, the best of the modern fairy tales reflect the complex problems brought about by

highly industrialized or post-industrial societies and the dif-
ficulties that the genre itself has in maintaining its utopian
purpose, for the fairy tale has always projected the wish and
possibility for human autonomy and eros and proposed
means to alter the world. As Michel Butor has remarked
about the images conveyed by the ideal and serious fairy
tale, "A world inverted, an exemplary world, fairyland is a
criticism of ossified reality. It does not remain side by side
with the latter; it reacts upon it; it suggests that we transform it, that we reinstate what is out of place."[2]

One of the qualitatively distinguishing features of the
fairy tale in America during the last decades of the twentieth century has been the manner in which it has questioned gender roles and critiqued the patriarchal code that
has been so dominant in both folk and fairy tales until the
1960s.[3] However, just as feminisms and the feminist movement have been culturally exploited and compromised by
the mass media and turned against themselves, the fairy tale
that seeks to maintain its utopian purpose and social critique is always in danger of being defused and transformed
into mere entertainment.

The quandary of the fairy tale was most evident during
the Reagan/Bush years of the 1980s, which brought a destruction of social welfare services and projects, increased
pauperization of women and minority groups, and support
for the individual self-absorption of the middle classes, often equated with the so-called Yuppies. It would appear
that the fairy tale in the 1980s became nothing more than a
decorative ornament, designed to titillate and distract readers and viewers, no matter how it was transformed as novel,
poem, short story, Broadway play, film, cassette, or TV series. Yet, it would be unfair to the fairy-tale genre and to the
writers of fairy tales to dismiss all the creative attempts as
mere decoration and a reflection of the narcissism of the
1980s. In some respects, the fairy tale can be characterized
as trying to find an adequate fantastical form to reply to the

curtailment of the fantasy in reality and to provide a viable option that will give audiences hope that they can reach their creative potential.

One of the more successful Broadway musicals toward the end of the 1980s was a production entitled *Into the Woods* (1987), which was a hodgepodge of various fairy tales that harmlessly poked fun at various fairy-tale characters like Little Red Riding Hood and was conceived mainly for commercial success.[4] Indeed, it was a success, and there has been something like a fairy-tale resurgence during the late 1980s that one could possibly interpret as a flight from reality, a withdrawal from the problems of American society, or more positively, a postmodernist endeavor to explore possibilities to go beyond the traditional boundaries of the fairy tale and generate new worlds. The fairy-tale TV series *Beauty and the Beast*, which ran from 1987 to 1990, had a large following in the States and has been successful as a rerun on TV and marketed as video. (And most likely the Disney Studio decided to capitalize on this popularity by producing its animated version of *Beauty and the Beast* along with a bestselling book in 1991.) Various fairy-tale films like *The Princess Bride* (1987) based on William Goldman's novel, have been popular in the theaters. Terri Windling began editing a series of novels that retell classic fairy tales at Ace Books in 1986, and six works by well-known fantasy authors have been published thus far. Numerous innovative illustrated fairy-tale books for children are issued each year, perhaps the most famous by Maurice Sendak entitled *Mili* (1988), based on a letter written by Wilhelm Grimm, which has sold over 200,000 copies. Moreover, the classical Grimm and Perrault fairy tales such as *The Frog Prince, Little Red Riding Hood, Snow White, Cinderella, Sleeping Beauty*, and others are newly illustrated and published in the thousands each year, often with cassettes or records. Finally, there are various fairy-tale imports from England and the Continent like the works of Michael Ende, Angela Carter, and Tanith Lee that are avidly read and seen by American audiences. For instance, Ende's *Neverending Story* (1984) was made into two films just as Carter's story "The Company of Wolves" from *Bloody Chamber* (1979) was adapted for the cinema.

In sum, the fairy tale has assumed many guises in America and is alive and well. That is, it is certainly immensely popular, but is it popular for the wrong reasons? Is the hope it promises perverse? Does it offer temporary escape from the hard times of the present? Is there anything of substance in the fairy-tale experimentation that sets a foundation for essential cultural transformation?

There are no definitive answers to these questions, and it is extremely difficult to provide a comprehensive picture of the different types of fairy-tale experimentation that are presently being undertaken in different medias today. Nevertheless, some key works—Maurice Sendak's *Mili* (1988), the TV series *Beauty and the Beast*, William Goldman's *The Princess Bride*, Raymond E. Feist's *Faerie Tale* (1988), Wendy Walker's *The Sea-Rabbit, or The Artist of Life* (1988), Jane Yolen's *Tales of Wonder* (1983), six fairy-tale novels by Steven Brust, Kara Dalkey, Charles de Lint, Patricia C. Wrede, Pamela Dean, and Jane Yolen in Terri Windling's series, and Robert Coover's "The Gingerbread House" (1970)—can help us at least address some of the questions I raised, for they are representative of both regressive and progressive tendencies to make the genre play a vital role in the development in American culture.

The history behind *Mili* is highly significant because it reveals something about the connections between production, reception, and form of children's fairy tales in the late 1980s. In 1983 Justin Schiller, a well-known New York bookseller, auctioned off a letter written by Wilhelm Grimm that contained a trite and sentimental tale. When the bidding contest was over, Michael di Capua of Farrar, Straus and Giroux boasted that he had paid well over the $26,000 asking price. In order to recoup his money di Capua announced to the press that the unknown alleged "magnificent" tale would be translated by the gifted Ralph Mannheim and illustrated by the famous Maurice Sendak. Now, this tale was written by Wilhelm in a letter to a girl named Mili, evidently to give her some solace during the Napoleonic Wars. The tale itself was not original but part of a didactic religious tradition and was fully developed by Wilhelm in a different way in "St. Joseph in the Woods" in the second edition of the Grimms' *Kinder- und Hausmärchen* (1819). The fact that Wilhelm never felt the need to refer to the "Mili tale" later in his work on folk tales is indicative of his low opinion of this trite piece. The plot is simple: a mother sends her daughter into the woods in order to save her from an encroaching war, and she tells her to trust in God. The obedient and pious child does as she is told and is protected by a guardian angel. In the woods she finds an old man who is actually St. Joseph, and she shows how domesticated she is by performing various humble acts. After thirty years of dutiful behavior, which the girl perceives as only three years, she is sent home by St. Joseph, who gives her a rose to carry to her mother. When the girl is reunited with her, they go to sleep and are found dead the next morning with St. Joseph's rose in full bloom.

Anyone familiar with Sendak's work, particularly *Where the Wild Things Are*, can perhaps understand why he was drawn to this tale. He has never tired of illustrating the flight and return of the child, who reconciles himself to a mother or home. However, rarely in his career has he ever illustrated a text so dripping with religious sentiment as this one. Where, then, is the book's salvation if there is one? In reading it as my daughter did when she could not read. That is, to ignore the text and look at Sendak's playful pastel illustrations that recall the odyssey of a courageous girl who survives on her own in a mysterious forest. In fact, Sendak unconsciously or consciously re-illustrates the history of Little Red Riding Hood in a fascinating way.

Sendak's girl, who cannot be more than eight, is adorned
with a red frock, and throughout the illustrations Sendak
uses all sorts of hues of red to play upon the theme of courage and/or sin. Clearly, his little girl, who loses her red
shoes in the woods and who will return barefoot to her
mother with a red rose, blossoms as the images of the
woods are transformed from wilderness to garden of Eden.
As usual, Sendak has his fun with his viewers by introducing personal themes and motifs from his other works. For
instance, Mozart, also dressed in a red jacket, conducts a
choir of Brooklyn school kids in one scene. In another, St.
Joseph, who looks more like an old wise rabbi than a Christian saint, gives the rose to the girl as a sign of redemption.
The man in the woods is not a wolf but a spiritual guide,
who looks after her during a period of trial and separation.

Unfortunately, most of the illustrations are derivative and
bland. In the final analysis, the text of *Dear Mili*, seen
through the eyes of Maurice Sendak, is transformed into another story that has something to do with Maurice Sendak's
personal odyssey and sentimental old age. Gone is the rebel-
lion of his early period. Gone are the weird disturbing figures
of *The Juniper Tree*. Sendak has tamed himself, and though
Dear Mili may be sweet and tender, it reflects a restorative
tendency of the contemporary American fairy tale for children. Obedience to the mother, diligence, submission to male
authority, reward by divine powers—these are the dominant
motifs in a fairy tale that does not show respect for the
autonomy of a child or encourage her to develop her creative powers. Such a tale is perfectly in accord with the present ideological atmosphere in America, and it is not much
different from most of the reprints of the Grimm's classical
tales. Of course, there are numerous endeavors to rewrite
and re-illustrate the traditional tales such as Shirley Climo's
The Egyptian Cinderella (1989), Charlotte Huck's *Princess
Furball* (1989), and Margot Tomes's *Tattercoats* (1989).
Most of these tales depict a strong heroine who actively

determines her own destiny. Yet, despite the strong feminist component in many of the new and revised fairy tales for children, the emphasis on closure, harmony, happy end, and a well-ordered world remains the governing principle so that the tales rarely hold a critical mirror to the ossified reality of our times. In the case of fairy tales for children, the harmonious ends may be justified as long as they motivate children to believe that sex roles can be altered. But, given the vast problems confronting women in American society—teenage pregnancy, pauperization of single women with children, inequitable wages—these fairy tales also conceal reality and give children a false impression of what awaits them as they mature.

This is not to say that there have not been revisions of classical fairy tales for children that compel readers to confront the harsh realities of the 1980s.[5] Martin Waddell's *The Touch Princess* (1986) and Babbette Cole's *Princess Smartypants* (1986)[6] are superb examples of how writers and illustrators can revise the classical tradition in a way that can contribute to the autonomy of children. Both are parodies of *King Thrushbeard* or *The Taming of the Shrew* and present young women who resist the will of their parents who want them to marry the perfect prince. These tales, told with delightful and unorthodox images, are open-ended and provoke readers to reconsider their gender identity with the hope that they can become who they want to be. There are, however, radical revisions of fairy tales that leave shockingly little hope. For intance, the theme of violence, the violation of a child's will, is treated in a more somber way in Sarah Moon's remarkable *Little Red Riding Hood*. Using Charles Perrault's 1697 text with her own stark, contemporary photographs of a young girl on her way to her grandmother's house at night in an urban setting, Moon addresses the topic of violence in our society and shifts the blame for the girl's rape and/or death to the predators or to social conditions. This revised version of *Little Red Riding Hood* is a haunting photographic essay about the danger girls face in our streets. Not only do the photos demand that we reexamine Perrault's text carefully, they also make us aware of the insidious threatening climate in which young girls grow up with dread.

Apparently this was also the intention of the TV series *Beauty and the Beast*, conceived in 1986 by Ron Koslow and adapted as a fairy-tale novel by Barbara Hambly in 1989.[7] The plot tells all: Catherine Chandler, daughter of a wealthy corporate lawyer, has followd her father's footsteps, and after graduating Radcliffe and Cornell Law School, she works in his New York office as an associate. Though not satisfied with her work, Catherine enjoys the glitter of New York and lives the life of a professional Yuppie. She mixes mainly with the rich, and her lover, Tom Gunther, an ambitious real estate developer, is concerned primarily with prestige and money, values that Catherine appears to share. Indeed, she could be described as a spoiled New York princess, who has no awareness of the social problems in New York. However, one night she is kidnapped, raped, and beaten. Left for dead in Central Park, she is found by a strange beastly creature named Vincent, who is from an underground world. A cross between a lion and human, Vincent was found as a baby by an extraordinary man named Father, who raised him in the underground tunnels of New York, where numerous homeless people and outcasts live. These people are the "different" ones, the nonconformists with a heart, who have rejected the capitalist society of New York and are content to live in the tunnels from the remnants discarded every day by the New Yorkers.

After Catherine spends ten days with Vincent, who helps her recuperate from her attack, she returns to the city with a completely different consciousness. She leaves her father's firm and begins working for the district attorney's office to help the victims of social injustice. Moreover, she breaks her relationship with Tom and feels a deep bond of affinity and love for Vincent, who is dedicated to preserving the underground world that has a precarious existence. Though Catherine and Vincent rarely see each other, they feel each other's presence all the time. Finally, when Catherine, who has learned self-defense, tracks down her kidnappers, who run a prostitution and blackmail racket, she valiantly fights them but appears to be doomed. Suddenly, Vincent appears out of nowhere to kill the thugs and rescue Catherine. Though they must part again, Catherine "had no idea where this would end, no idea where it might lead her. She only knew that they were bound together, she and this strange and beautiful soul, and the thought, rather than uncertainty, brought her peace."[8]

This fairy-tale novel is based the two-hour TV pilot that introduced the series in 1987. The ending of the novel, like the TV pilot, had to be inconclusive so that Catherine and Vincent could have many adventures for the next two TV seasons with the pair taking turns saving each other and developing a more passionate love. Both the novel and TV series are based on sentimental and predictable plots. The appeal of both, however, can be attributed to the fact that Koslow employed a well-known fairy-tale scheme to address immediate problems of American society, ranging from drugs to white collar crimes. Moreover, here it is the princess who is converted into a more humane person by the beast, who remains a beast and true to his outsider state. Another appealing factor was the unconsummated love between Catherine and Vincent. Unfortunately, the series quickly succumbed to the stale formula of most crime shows on American TV and did not develop the fairy-tale form in a new way, and the novel is written in a trite, traditional manner that leaves little room for the reader's imagination.

William Goldman's *The Princess Bride*, published as a novel in 1973 and produced as a film in 1987, is a mock fairy tale that plays with traditional motifs and themes and that challenges the reader/viewer to consider whether fairy tales have any value for us today. In the comic introduction to the book, Goldman tells the reader how his father, a European immigrant, used to read S. Morgenstern's classic fairy tale, *The Princess Bride*, with the boring parts left out. Since it was his favorite book, Goldman writes his own adaptation for contemporary readers and retells the tale, constantly interrupting the flow of the narrative with droll comments.

The story concerns the beautiful Buttercup in the land of Florin somewhere between Sweden and Germany some time long ago. Buttercup is a feisty village maid who always orders the farm boy Westly to do all the chores, until she reaches eighteen and realizes she loves him. However, he decides to go to America and find his fortune there to be worthy of her love. While he is gone for three years, Buttercup is forced to become engaged to Prince Humperdinck of Florin, who eventually wants her murderd by three unusual villains, Inigo the greatest swordsman in the world, Fezzik the strongest man in the world, and Vizzini, the cruelest man in the world. However, Westley returns in disguise and outsmarts these villains, and later two of them join him and help him rescue Buttercup from the evil designs of the prince. Nobody is what he or she appears in this fairy tale. The characters speak in contemporary American slang. The impossible is always possible. In the end, Goldman leaves the reader up in the air as to whether Buttercup and Westley will live happily ever after. In his opinion, after they escaped, "they squabbled a lot, and Buttercup lost her looks eventually, and one day Fezzik lost a fight and some hotshot kid whipped Inigo with a sword and Westley was never able to really sleep sound because of Humperdinck maybe being on the trail. I'm not trying to make this a downer, understand. I mean, I really do think that love is the best thing in the world, except for cough drops. But I also have to say, for the umpty-umpth time, that life isn't fair. It's just fairer than death, that's all." [9]

Entertaining and bizarre, this novel parodies all the conventions of the fairy tale but not with the intention to dismiss the value of the genre. Goldman recreates himself as the fictitious author of this work; that is, he uses a mask in the tradition of eighteenth-century novels and recalls how his father's telling of Morgenstern's fairy tale introduced him to a new world of fantasy that cured him of a sickness, somewhat like Michael Ende's *Neverending Story*, and that this imaginative story remained with him because it changed his life. In other words, the power of the imagination can cause changes in reality and alter one's life.

However, imagination and creativity have been on the defensive for some time now, and most of the recent fairy-tale novels record in some form of another the desperate fight of valiant heroes and heroines to save the imagination from being destroyed or wiped out by the instrumental forces of technology that seek to rationalize life in a sterile and exploitative manner. It is not by chance then that the series of fairy-tale novels edited by Terri Windling has as its major purpose to breathe new life into traditional material and show the diverse uses a modern storyteller can make out of the fairy-tale genre. The first six novels in the series appear to be manifestoes in defense of the power of the imagination.

Steven Brust's *The Sun, the Moon, and the Stars* (1987) is based on a Hungarian folk tale and set in contemporary America. A group of artists work together in a studio and appear doomed to obscurity. However, they fight against odds to arrange for an exhibition and gain respect for their imaginative endeavors. In Charles de Lint's *Jack the Giant Killer* (1987), he borrows from folk tales about cunning tailors and tricksters to weave together his own fantastic narrative about a young woman, named Jacky, whose mundane life is suddenly transformed in an extraordinary way. She witnesses the mysterious murder of a tiny man called a hob in the city of Ottawa. Soon she feels compelled to explore this mystery, and before Jacky knows it, she becomes the only hope of a fairy realm called Kinrowan threatened by savage hordes. With the help of her best friend Kate (Crackernuts) Hazel and a swanlike prince, she demonstrates that force and violence are not necessary to overcome brutality if one has faith in the imagination. This message is also stressed in Pamela Dean's *Tam Lin* (1991), which is actually a fairy-tale adaptation of an old Scottish ballad. She, too, updates the ballad to the Vietnam era and sets the action at a Midwestern college, where Janet, her pregnant heroine, must make a difficult decision about "keeping the heart of flesh in a world that wants to put in a heart of stone." [10]

In contrast to the contemporary settings of Dean, Brust, and de Lint, Kara Dalkey's *The Nightingale* (1988) and Patricia C. Wrede's *Snow White and Rose Red* (1989) take place in the past. Dalke's revision of Hans Christian Andersen's tale is set in medieval Japan and concerns Uguisu, who uses her extraordinary talent as a flutist, to save the emperor's life and bring about peace and harmony in his kingdom. Wrede's adaptation of Wilhelm Grimm's *Snow White and Rose Red* takes place in Elizabethan England. Unlike Grimm's version, the Widow Arden and her two daughters, Blanche and Rosamund, are active and creative characters, who help the queen of faerie and her two half-mortal sons, Hugh and John, to keep the ties alive between the fairy realm and mundane society.

The most recent of the fairy-tale novels in the Windling series, Jane Yolen's *Briar Rose* (1992), is by far the most experimental. It moves through memory, flashbacks, and a retelling of "Sleeping Beauty" from the present to the horrors of the Holocaust. In her haunting narrative that reads somewhat like a mystery novel, Yolen demonstrates that fairy tales can be used to address the most atrocious crimes of the Nazi period in a manner that generates hope in readers who, Yolen believes, must come to terms with Auschwitz and its consequences.

Though the plots of each one of these novels that I have discussed are certainly very different, there is a common thread that unites them, a thread that can be traced back to German romanticism and especially the works of E.T.A. Hoffmann: there is a secret humane and imaginative world, the realm of faerie, that is threatened by powermongers, rationalists, materialists, scientists, and the like. Without this world, i.e., without imagination, life would become drab and monotonous, and people would become like automatons. Somehow a balance must be struck between the inner and outer worlds of human beings, between the creative forces of the imagination and the reality principle of the world.

This message is at the heart of a bestseller entitled simply *Faerie Tale* by Raymond E. Feist. The plot concerns a successful screenwriter by the name of Phil Hasting, who moves into a huge house in rural upstate New York with his wife and three children. However, it turns out that the house is the seat of magic powers, and a magic black force is accidentally unleashed by Hasting and his friends. The Queen of faerie and her realm become endangered, and Hasting's twin sons are on the brink of death because an agreement between the guardians of faerie power has been broken by one of its members. Fortunately, the sons, who believe in the faerie power, have the courage to resist the evil forces, and they are all saved by the intervention of the guardians of the faerie realm.

Feist's novel contains long-winded expositions about magic, Celtic tradition, and fairies and has a secondary plot concerned with Hasting's teenage princess daughter, a rich heiress, who falls in love with an All-American graduate student writing his dissertation on a topic related to the occult and magic. Like the other fairy-tale novels, this plot is strained and at times preposterous and pretentious. The best that one can say about the lot of them is that they want to find an adequate form for the fairy tale so that it can

maintain its critical and utopian function—to hold a mirror
to ossified reality and to suggest imaginative ways to alter
our lives.

Whereas the longer narrative forms of the fairy tale, i.e.,
the fairy-tale novel, tend to be too predictable and unimag-
inative in their endeavors to protect the imagination from
the encroachment of rationalism, the contemporary writers
of short fairy tales appear to be more effective in their experiments. Here the works of Wendy Walker, Jane Yolen,
and Robert Coover are good examples of the different ways
contemporary American writers are experimenting with
short prose fairy tales.

In *The Sea-Rabbit, or The Artist of Life* (1988) Walker
has rewritten six tales from the Grimms' *Children's and
Household Tales*, composed two new stories about Samson
and Delilah and the woman who lived in a boot, and invented a parable about the cathedral of Notre Dame, all
with the purpose of altering our customary notions about
the classical fairy-tale tradition and the real-life conflicts
within it. She accomplishes her modernist goal of restoring
the unspoken of the traditional tales by fleshing out the
lives of the original characters, probing their psyches, and
altering narrative perspectives.

In the title tale of the book, "The Sea Rabbit," based on
the Grimms' "The Little Hamster from the Water," she presents an unlikely protagonist who refuses to accept the role
of hero, for he is not particularly enamored of the cruel and
haughty princess, who takes pleasure in cutting off the heads
of her suitors if they are not smart enough to deceive her and
find a hiding place that she is unable to discover. Despite the
fact that he outwits her and "wins" her, he is not optimistic
about the future, given the princess's former predilection. In
"Ashipattle," Walker's version of "Cinderella," the prince
expresses his disappointment after marrying Ashipattle, who
becomes concerned mainly with building a bird-castle for
her beloved birds. Walker's other characters, Clever Elsie,

Jack My Hedgehog, the discharged soldier from "The Worn-Out Dancing Shoes," and Arnaud, the hunter from the Grimms' tales, also have strange fates that alienate us from our typical expectations, for they refuse to settle for material wealth and superficial happiness.

Although Walker sometimes remains too close to the original plotlines of the Grimms' tales, her terse style and use of different narrative voices produce haunting images that fuse the past with the present. She is relentlessly blunt when it comes to exploring the psychological truths of the old tales, as though she wants to expose the way we have been blinded by the traditional fairy tales. Her tales do not provide "happy" or cathartic relief for readers, rather they are startling and troubling, and in this sense they renew the fairy-tale tradition by undermining the authoritative voice of the Grimms' tradition and exposing problems that are directly related to our present troubled times and cannot be easily resolved.

Transforming the traditional fairy tales into problems without solutions has been a major goal of Jane Yolen, who has been writing unique fairy tales for children and adults for the past twenty years. The best examples of her work can be found in her book *Tales of Wonder* (1983) and *Dragonfield and Other Stories* (1985). She has consistently experimented with the fairy-tale genre in a twofold manner by revising traditional tales with an eye toward exploring their psychological undercurrents and by creating her own unusual tales that fuse motifs and themes from the fairy-tale tradition and fantasy literature. As Patricia McKillip has remarked, "her stories make no promises, guarantee no happy endings. They present worlds which alter under our eyes like the shapes of clouds. Image flows into image: the tree becomes a lover, the ribbon of gray hair becomes a silver road out of torment, the tears become like flowers, the old drunk on the beach becomes the god of the sea. Each image is a gift without explanation." [11]

Among the best of her revised "classical" fairy tales are
"The Moon Ribbon," "Brother Hart," "The Thirteenth
Fay," "Happy Dens or A Day in the Old Wolves Home,"
and "The Undine," which are characterized by plots that
compel readers to ponder their traditional expectations and
by unique metaphors that give rise to startling images. For
instance, in "The Undine" she emphasizes the notion of
male betrayal and female autonomy in an implicit critique
of Hans Christian Andersen's "The Little Mermaid." Here
the mermaid leaves the prince, who beckoned her, to return
to her sisters in the sea that "opened to her, gathered her in,
washed her clean." [12] In "The Thirteenth Fey," Yolen recalls
the story of "Sleeping Beauty" through a first-person narrative of the youngest daughter of a family of fairies, who tells
us, "we owe our fortunes, our existence, and the lives of our
children to come to the owners of that land. We are bound
to do them duty, we women of the fey.. and during all the
time of our habitation, the local lords have been a dynasty
of idiots, fornicators, louts, greedyguts, and fools." [13]

What follows is an amusing parody of the decadent monarchy. The youngest fairy, who cannot stand the royal family, makes a mistake at the birth of Thalia, causing her to
sleep a hundred years. But the fairy considers her mistake
most fortunate for her family, for she has been studying
history and has discovered that there will be a

rise of a religion called Democracy which believes in neither mon-
archs nor magic. It encourages the common man. When, in a hundred years, some young princeling manages to unravel the knot of
wood about Talia's domain, I plan to be by his side, whispering
the rote of revolution in his ear. If my luck holds . . . Talia will
seem to him only a rustic relic of a bygone era whose bedclothes
speak of decadence and whose bubbly breath of decay he will wed
out of compassion, and learn Computer Science. Then the spell of
the land will be broken. No royal wedding—no royal babes. No
babes—no inheritance. And though we fey will still be tied to the
land, our wishes will belong to us alone.[14]

The various narrative voices employed by Yolen have a definite feminist bias without being didactic or dogmatic. Like Angela Carter and Tanith Lee, one of her major achievements has been to subvert the male-discourse that has dominated the fairy tale as genre so that the repressed concerns of women are addressed, and the predictable happy ends that signify male hegemony and closure are exploded or placed into question. Thus, in "The White Seal Maid" and "The Lady and the Merman," she has her female protagonists seek refuge in their origins, the sea, which represent for Yolen the essence of restlessness, change, tenderness, and humanity.

Overall, Yolen's tales have been strongly influenced by contemporary social, political, and aesthetic movements. In fact, her experiments with the fairy tale seem to reflect the manner in which Americans have been struggling for more equitable sexual and social relations. On the aesthetic level, her fairy-tale revisions may be associated with what Cristina Bacchilega has defined as "the strategies post-modern writers engage in to expose, question, and re-create the rules of narrative production." [15] According to Bacchilega, the characteristic features of postmodernism are "the pastiche, the schizophrenic de-realization and intensification of the world, the fragmentation and flatness of representation, the ensuing suspicion of concepts such as truth and identity, the immersion in a fast-paced, city-world of consumerism, and the lack of a positive or negative norm to refer to." [16]

These elements can be found in the works of Donald Barthelme, Robert Coover, and Angela Carter, who break down the conventions of the classical fairy-tale narrative, in order to alter our readings of the privileged narratives that have formed a type of canon in Western culture. The postmodern revisions, however, do not reassemble the fairy tales that they break down into fragments into a new whole. Instead, they expose the artifice of the fairy tale and make us aware that there are different ways to shape and view the stories. The end goal of the postmodernist fairy tale is not closure but openness, not recuperation but differentiation, not the establishment of a new norm but the questioning of all norms.

A good example of this type of writing is Robert Coover's "The Gingerbread House" which appeared in *Pricksongs and Descants* in 1970 and is a revision of the Grimms' "Hansel and Gretel." Coover breaks down the narrative into forty-two frames and begins the story in media res: "A pine forest in the midafternoon. Two children follow an old man, dropping breadcrumbs, singing nursery tunes. Dense earthy greens seep into the darkening distance, flecked and streaked with filtered sunlight. Spots of red, violet, pale blue, gold, burnt orange. The girl carries a basket for gathering flowers. The boy is occupied with the crumbs. Their song tells of God's care for little ones."[17] What ensues is a trip through the woods filled with tension but never explained. For instance, in the seventh frame, we read that "the old man's gaze is straight ahead, but at what? Perhaps at nothing. Some invisible destination. Some irrecoverable point of departure."[18] Only one thing is clear: this is a tale in which the introductory song and the Grimms' paradigm no longer hold true. There will be no God's care for little ones, nor will there be a happy reconciliation with the parents.

As the children move through the woods, they fight over an injured dove and are abandoned by their miserable father. Meanwhile the witch, who has torn out the heart of a dove, awaits them. Images of dread and doom are contrasted with the bright and appealing gingerbread house. In the end, we are left at the entrance to the house: "But the door: here they pause and catch their breath. It is heart-shaped and blood-stone-red, its burnished surface gleaming in the sunlight. Oh, what a thing is that door! Shining like a ruby, like hard cherry candy, and pulsing softly, radiantly. Yes, marvelous! insuperable! but beyond: what is that sound of black rags flapping?"[19]

Coover takes away the hope of the traditional "Hansel

and Gretel," and leaves us as he began—in media res. To understand the voyage we must go back and reread or follow the footsteps of the two children. We are left paused on a threshold. Are the children going to be treated like the two doves in the story? Is there no hope for the doves? We know what happens in the old narrative, but will it be possible, once the two unnamed children cross the threshold, to escape and return home? Why return home? Unlike the classical fairy tale, we are left with questions and a state of uncertainty. What was once the primary function or the utopian function of the fairy tale—to provide hope—has been undermined. Here its main purpose is to hold a cracked mirror up to the old fairy tales and reality at the same time.

However, Coover's postmodern fairy tale and those by Bartheleme, Carter, Yolen, Atwood, and others are *not* typical of the major endeavors of contemporary American writers. Most provide closure of one kind or another; most retain a strong element of hope, especially the longer fiction. Nevertheless, more than the other contemporary types, the postmodern fairy tale does bring out the major characteristic of the best of contemporary American fairy tales: the self-reflective search for a fantastical form that will recuperate the utopian function of the traditional fairy tale in a manner that is commensurate with the major social changes in the postindustrial world.

What characteristics can be distinguished in the contemporary fairy tale in America and what tendencies can be expected in the future?

1. Continued re-production and duplication of the classical fairy tales for children and adults as a "natural" function of the culture industry that seeks to preserve the classical literary canon without questioning it. Here the Disney studio continues to exercise a great influence. Even with its "feminist" slant, the Disney *Beauty and the Beast* is basically a duplication of a traditional tale and follows the usual prescriptives of the Hollywood and Broadway musical.

2. Parodies and revisions of the classical fairy tale in various forms—TV commercials, films, literature—to provide entertainment, to question convention, and to signal something new through a familiar signifier. Here Tom Davenport's cinematic productions "Ashpet," "Soldier Jack," and "Hansel and Gretel," which have an Appalachian setting, are interesting experiments.[20] In addition, Ellen Datlow and Terri Windling have edited an anthology entitled *Snow White, Blood Red* (1993), which contains twenty new versions with classical fairy tales, some highly provocative and some that are trivial.

3. Feminist fairy tales that subvert the male discourse and patriarchal ideology apparent in the traditional fairy tales by shifting the narrative voice, undoing plots, and expressing the concerns of women through new images and styles of writing. Here Robin Morgan's *The Mer-Child: A Legend for Children and Other Adults* (1991) is a remarkable feminist subversion of Andersen's *The Little Mermaid*. The tale concerns a little girl, who is the daughter of a black mother and a white father. Since she has been ostracized because of her race and because her legs are paralyzed, she spends a great deal of time alone by the sea, where she meets a green Mer-Child, an alien creature, whose otherness empowers the girl so that, unlike in Andersen's tale, she learns to walk and take control of her life.

4. Straightforward utopian revisions of classical fairy tales and melanges that borrow from fantasy fiction and science fiction seek to *defend* the imagination and the humane spirit in a neoromantic protest against rationalization and instrumentalization in capitalist societies. Here Salman Rushdie's *Haroun and the Sea of Stories* (1990) is a good example of how a fairy-tale novel can incorporate a critique of tyranny with a utopian treatise about the meaningfulness of storytelling. There are also some interesting utopian tales in *Once Upon a Time: A Treasury of Modern Fairy Tales* (1990), edited by Lester Del Rey and Risa Kessler, but for the most part the authors demean utopia with hackneyed treatments of the fairy tale.[21]

5. Postmodern experiments that interrogate the way the world has been presented in fairy tales and the way we read fairy tales by forming pastiches and abstractions, difficult to decipher and open to various interpretations. Coover's latest fairy-tale novel,

Pinocchio in Venice (1991), a flawed tour de force, is a good example here.

Clearly, one cannot speak about *the* fairy tale in America today, or *the* American fairy tale. The most crucial question, however, for the genre as a whole, including all the different media types, is whether it can truly recapture its credible utopian function. And, of course, the answer to this question depends on whether we can realistically conceive of utopias in a world where chaos, poverty, war, and exploitation take precedence over our dreams, and when there is a danger that we will now conceive of false utopias after the momentous changes that have occurred in Eastern Europe, Africa, and the Middle East. Indeed, it has become apparent that the American concept of the "free world" cannot be easily exported, and peace and harmony cannot be easily attained. Yet, despite the fact that conflicts have continued at home and abroad, they serve a positive function, for they compel us to rethink the meaning of utopia and freedom in reality and in the realm of the fairy tale as well. And as we move into the twenty-first century and continue to talk about shaping a new world order, the utopian verve of the American fairy tale will certainly play a role in designating imaginative directions as correctives to the political shortcomings of our politicians and statesmen. In this respect, though there may not be an *American* fairy tale, American writers of fairy tales have already distinguished themselves by keeping alive alternatives for a better future in their innovative narratives that refuse to make compromises with the mythicization of the classical tradition.

NOTES

INTRODUCTION

1. Trs. Willard R. Task (New York): Harper and Row, 1963), 195-202.

2. Eliade reviewed Jan de Vries's *Betrachtungen zum Märchen, besonders in seinem Verhältnis zu Heldensage und Mythos* (1954) in *La Nouvelle Revue Française* in May, 1956, and used the opportunity to elaborate his ideas about myths and fairy tales.

3. *Ibid.*, 5-6

4. *Ibid.*, 196-97.

5. *Ibid.*, 201.

6. *Ibid.*, 202.

7. London: Granada, 1973.

8. New York: Hill and Wang, 1977.

9. "Change the Object Itself: Mythology Today" in *Image—Music—Text* (New York: Hill and Wang, 1977), 165.

10. *Mythologies* 123.

11. *Ibid.*, 124.

12. *Ibid.*, 125.

13. William Little, *The Oxford Universal Dictionary* 3rd rev. ed. (Oxford: Oxford Univ. Press, 1955), 1728.

14. Cf. my essay, "The Rise of the French Fairy Tale and the Decline of France" in *Beauties, Beasts and Enchantment: Classic French Fairy Tales*, trs. Jack Zipes (New York: New American Library, 1989), 1-15.

15. See Straparola's *Le piacevoli notti* (1550-53), translated as

The Facetious Nights or *The Delectable Nights*, and Basile's *Lo Cunto de li Cunti* (*The Story of Stories*, 1634-36), better known as *The Pentamerone.* The Italians did not "institutionalize" the genre because the literary culture in Italy was not prepared to introduce the tales as part of the civilizing process, nor were there groups of writers who made the fairy-tale genre part of their discourse.

16. Cf. the different essays in Nancy Armstrong and Leonard Tennenhouse, eds., *The Violence of Representation: Literature and the History of Violence* (New York: Routledge, 1989).

17. *Ibid.*, 24.

18. Cf. *Die Domestizierte Phantasie: Studien zur Kinderliteratur, Kinderlektüre und Literaturpädagogik des 18. und frühen 19. Jahrhunderts* (Heidelberg: Carl Winter, 1987).

19. This list would include the Grimms, Wilhelm Hauff, Ludwig Bechstein, Hans Christian Andersen, Madame De Ségur, and numerous collections of expurgated folk tales from different countries that became popular in primers by the end of the nineteenth century. Here one would have to mention the series of color fairy books edited by Andrew Lang in Great Britian.

1. ORIGINS OF THE FAIRY TALE

1. "Toward Supreme Fictions," *Yale French Studies* 43 (1969): 11.

2. See also Philippe Ariès, "At the Point of Origin," *Yale French Studies* 43 (1969): 15-23.

3. In my book *Fairy Tales and the Art of Subversion* (London: Heinemann, 1983), I endeavored to trace the origins in relation to the civilizing process, and the present essay is an amplification of the ideas developed in my book.

4. Trs. Michael Shaw (Minneapolis: Univ. of Minnesota Press, 1984).

5. *Ibid.*, 12.

6. *Ibid.*, 48.

7. *Ibid.*, 47.

8. The following remarks are based to a large extent on Renate Baader's excellent study, *Dames de Lettres: Autorinnen des preziösen, hocharistokratischen und 'modernen' Salons (1649-1698): Mlle de Scudéry—Mlle de Montpensier—Mme d'Aulnoy* (Stuttgart:

Metzler, 1986). In particular, see "Mme d'Aulnoy und das feminine Salonmärchen (1697-1698)," 226-77.

9. Cf. Jacques Barchilon, *Le conte merveilleux français de 1690 à 1790* (Paris: Champion, 1975) and Raymonde Robert, *Le conte de fées littéraire en France de la fin du XVIIe à la fin du XVIIIe siècle* (Nancy: Presses Universitaires de Nancy, 1981).

10. See Hubert Gillot, *La Querelle des Anciens et des Modernes* (Geneva: Slatkine, 1968, reprint of 1914 edition) and the "Introduction" to Charles Perrault, *Memoirs of My Life*, ed. and trs. Jeanne Morgan Zarucchi (Columbia: Univ. of Missouri Press, 1989), 1-25.

11. *Ibid.*, 239.

12. For the most complete history of this development, see Betsy Hearne, *Beauty and the Beast: Visions and Revisions of an Old Tale* (Chicago: University of Chicago Press, 1989). I have also commented on this development in my book *Fairy Tales and the Art of Subversion* (London: Heinemann, 1983), 32-44.

13. "A French Writer and Educator in England: Mme Le Prince de Beaumont," *Studies on Voltaire and the Eighteenth Century* 201 (1982): 201-2.

14. "Beauty and the Beast" in *Beauties, Beasts and Enchantment: Classic French Fairy Tales*, trs. Jack Zipes (New York: NAL, 1989), 237.

15. "A French writer and Educator in England: Mme Le Prince de Beaumont," 198.

16. *The Bonds of Love: Psychoanalysis, Feminism, and the Problem of Domination* (New York: Pantheon, 1988), 136.

17. *Ibid.*, 168.

18. *Beauty and the Beast*, illustr. Alfred Crowquill (London: Orr, 1853).

19. In *Grimm Tales Made Gay*, illustr. Albert Levering (Boston: Houghton, Mifflin, 1902), 65-70. There is a wonderful moral to this poem that reads:

Predicaments often are found
That beautiful duty is apt to get round:
But greedy extortioners better beware
For dutiful beauty is apt to get square!

20. See *The Bloody Chamber and Other Stories* (London: Gollancz, 1979).

21. "Re-Constructing Oedipus Through 'Beauty and the Beast,'" *Criticism* 31 (Fall, 1989): 448.

22. In *Not Quite as Grimm* (London: Abelard-Schuman, 1974).

23. In *Beginning with O* (New Haven: Yale Univ. Press, 1977).

24. *A Retelling of the Story of Beauty and the Beast* (New York: Harper and Row, 1978).

25. In *Story Hour* (Fayeteville: Univ. of Arkansas Press, 1982).

26. In *Red as Blood, or Tales of the Sisters Grimmer.* (New York: DAW, 1983).

27. In *The One Who Set Out to Study Fear* (London: Bloomsbury, 1989).

28. In *Trail of Stones* (London: Julia MacRae Books, 1990).

29. See the interesting reprint, *Beauty and the Beast*, ed. Andrew Lang (London: Leadenhall Press, 1886).

30. (London: Routledge, 1875).

31. (London: Longmans, Green and Co., 1889).

32. (London: Hodder and Stoughton, 1910).

33. "*Beauty and the Beast*: From Fable to Film," *Film Quarterly* 17 (1989): 87.

34. Sylvia Bryant's remarks about Cocteau's sadistic treatment of Beauty in "Re-Constructing Oedipus Through 'Beauty and the Beast'" are very apropos:

This trade-off, Beast for Prince, which is effected without her consent, is explicit in the "happy ending" it intends. Her desires are, in fact, doubly discounted, for despite her requisite self-sacrifice, Beauty doesn't get what/whom she bargained for. The "Prince with three faces" with whom she flies away is a composite of the single, inescapable face of the patriarchal culture which has made her, inscribed her—Avenant, Beast, Prince Charming, father, lord. And even her physical presence as determinate of identity is compromised—indeed, revoked, for the last image the spectator sees is the prince's smiling face; Beauty's back, encircled by the Prince's arms, is turned to face the camera. In *La Belle et la Bête*, her story once again turns into his story; the narrative ending has been prestaged, pre-determined by the Oedipal constructs of the genre and the media even before the narrative discourse begins (445).

35. *The Virago Book of Fairy Tales*, ed. Angela Carter (London: Virago, 1990), xxi.

2. RUMPELSTILTSKIN

1. Folklorists have focused on tracing the origins of the name of Rumpelstiltskin and connecting the tale to legends about dwarfs and devils. See Edward Clodd, *Tim Tit Tot: An essay of Savage Philosophy* (London: 1898); Otto Kahn, "Rumpelstilz hat wirklich gelebt,"

Rheinisches Jahrbuch für Volkskunde 17/18 (1966/67): 143-84; Max Lüthi, "Rumpelstilzchen," *Antaios* 12 (1971): 419-36; and Howard Wright Marshall, "Tim Tit Tot: A Comparative Essay on Aarne-Thompson Type 500—The Name of the Helper," *Folklore* 84 (1973): 51-7. Psychoanalysts and psychological critics have generally emphasized the phallic aspects of Rumpelstiltskin or have interpreted it as a narrative of sexual anxiety, which the female character or analysand must learn to overcome. See Géza Roheim, "Tom, Tit, Tot," *Psychoanalytic Review* 36 (1949): 365-69; C.J. Schuurman, "The Psychoanalytical and the Psychosophical Interpretation of Fairy-Tales," *Folia Psychiatrica* 53 (1950): 509-18; Julius L. Rowley, "Rumpelstiltskin in the Analytical Situation," *International Journal of Psycho-Analysis* 32 (1951): 190-95; Charlotte Bühler and Josephine Bilz, *Das Märchen und die Phantasie des Kindes* (Munich: Nymphenburger Verlag, 1958): 103-9; Edmund Bergler, "The Clinical Importance of 'Rumpelstiltskin' as Anti-Male Manifesto," *American Imago* 18 (1961): Hedwig von Beit, *Symbolik des Märchens*, Vol. 2: *Gegensatz und Erneuerung im Märchen*, 2nd ed. (Bern: 1965): 535-43, 65-70; Leo Katz, "The Rumpelstiltskin Complex," *Contemporary Psychoanalysis* 10 (1974): 117-24; Donald B. Rinsely and Elizabeth Bergmann, "Enchantment and Alchemy: The Story of Rumpelstiltskin," *Bulletin of the Menniger Clinic* 47 (1983): 1-14; and Martin Miller, "Poor Rumpelstiltskin," *Psychoanalytic Quarterly* 54 (1985): 73-76. For a comprehensive view of the different approaches to *Rumpelstiltskin*, see Lutz Röhrich's stimulating essay "Rumpelstilzchen. Vom Methodenpluralismus in der Erzählforschung," in *Sage und Forschung: Erzählforschung heute* (Freiburg: Herder, 1976): 272-91. Even in his essay, however, spinning and the role of the spinner are not examined in depth.

2. This is not to say that the aspect of spinning has been totally neglected by scholars. As we shall see, Marianne Rumpf, Gerburg Treusch-Dieter, and Gonthier-Louis Fink make the issue of spinning the central theme of their research. My endeavor in this essay is to bring together their findings with a sharper focus on the sociohistorical reasons for the changes in *Rumpelstiltskin* and the transformation of female productivity.

3. Published in *La Tour Ténebreuse et Les Jours luminieux* (Paris: Barbin, 1705).

4. *Tim Tit Tot: An Essay of Savage Philosophy* (London: Duckworth, 1989), 36.

5. My translation of "Rumpenstünzchen" is from *Die älteste*

Märchensammlung der Brüder Grimm, ed. Heinz Rölleke (Cologny-Genève: Fondation Martin Bodmer, 1975), 238-40.

6. They mention it in the third volume of their notes, which they published in 1856: "The French *Ricdinricdon* in the *Tour tenébreuse* by Mlle L'héritier also belongs here, and there is a Danish version based on it." *Kinder und Hausmärchen gesammelt durch die Brüder Grimm*. vol. 3, 3rd ed. (Göttingen: Dietrich, 1856), 107. The Grimms allude to a few other literary versions in this note, indicating to what extent they took them into consideration while forming their final version of 1857.

7. See "Les Avatars de Rumpelstilzchen: La Vie d'un Conte Populaire" in *Deutsch-Französisches Gespräch im Lichte der Märchen* (Münster: Aschendorff, 1964), 63.

8. (Berlin: Ästhetik und Kommunikation, 1964), 12. The study includes a contribution by the sociologist Werner Siebel. In English translation, the title of the book announces Treusch-Dieter's major thesis: "How the Thread Was Taken Out of the Hands of Women: The Spindle of Necessity."

9. This point is also stressed in important books by Patricia Baines, *Spinning Wheels, Spinners & Spinning* (London: 1982); Marta Weigle, *Spiders and Spinsters: Woman and Mythology* (Albuquerque: Univ. of New Mexico Press, 1982); and Annette B. Weiner and Jane Schneider, *Cloth and Human Experience* (Washington D.C.: Smithsonian Institution Press, 1989).

10. *Wie den Frauen der Faden aus der Hand genommen wurde*, 19.

11. *Ibid.*, 19.

12. *Ibid.*, 20-21.

13. This is not to say that spinning was only the preoccupation of women. Men and children of both sexes did spinning, but the domain of spinning was considered a female vocation and dominated by women. It was through spinning that a young woman could prove her mettle and win a husband. See John Horner, *The Linen Trade of Europe During the Spinning-Wheel Period* (Belfast: M'Caw, Stevenson, and Orr, 1920) and Jane Schneider, "Rumpelstiltskin's Bargain: Folklore and the Merchant Capitalist Intensification of Linen Manufacture in Early Modern Europe," in *Cloth and Human Experience*, eds. Annette B. Weiner and Jane Schneider (Washington D.C.: Smithsonian Institution Press, 1989), 177-213.

14. Commenting on spinning in households of sixteenth-century Lyon, Natalie Zemon Davis remarks,

what we seem to have here is a domestic work culture, hidden from the streets, elicting comment not from city councils, but from storytellers. It drew on certain general features of a woman's life, as adaptable to spinning as to any other setting where women were working together, in contrast to "ancient customs," connected with the technology of a particular craft, which one might find in a shop dominated by men. The domestic work culture provided a kind of vertical identity between mistress and female worker, which could sometimes be used by the former to hurry along the work process and sometimes by the latter to slow it down. It was available to any woman—at least to any Catholic woman—who wanted to impose a rhythm on her life.

See "Women in the Crafts in Sixteenth-Century Lyon" *Feminist Studies* 8 (Spring, 1982): 62.

15. "Village Spinning Bees: Sexual Culture and Free Time Among Rural Youth in Early Modern Germany," in *Interest and Emotion: Essays on the Study of Family and Kinship*, ed. Hans Medick and David Warren Sabean (Cambridge: Cambridge Univ. Press, 1984), 329-31.

16. See Marianne Rumpf, "Spinnerinnen und Spinnen: Märchendeutungen aus kulturhistorischer Sicht," in *Die Frau im Märchen*, eds. Sigrid Früh and Rainer Wehse (Kassel: Erich Röth, 1985), 65.

17. See Hans Medick, "Village Spinning Bees in Early Modern Germany," 334-35.

The youth met in a completely different style. Their meetings drew their tension right from the beginning from the "play between the two sexes". Already in the early part of the evening in those Spinnstuben, in which girls and boys gathered separately, the expectation and the knowledge of the later coming together determined the contents and the rhythm of the sociability. Here there were specific differences between both sexes. The social forms of the female Spinnstube were not hierarchical. "In these assemblies there is simply no order of rank." The sociability is determined at the beginning by the work of spinning and the exchange over "matters of family and village". Later, songs and traditional stories take over.

18. *Ibid.*, 70.

19. *Wie den Frauen der Faden aus der hand genommen wurde*, 35.

20. "Rumpelstiltskin's Bargain," 206.

21. (Oxford: Oxford Univ. Press, 1944), 1971.

22. In fact, this tale is the earliest document that we have of the *Rumpelstiltskin* plot as produced by the Grimms, indicating that the

origins of this tale type may be found in literature and in the high regard that upper-class French women had toward spinning and cloth.

23. See "The Cloak," Trs. Jeannine Blackwell in *Bitter Healing: German Women Writers from 1700 to 1830*, eds. Jeannine Blackwell and Susanne Zantop (Lincoln: Univ. of Nebraska Press, 1990), 203-77. The German original, "Der kurze Mantel," appeared in *Neue Volksmährchen der Deutschen* (Leipzig: Weygand, 1789-92).

24. Cf. Ruth B. Bottigheimer, "Tale Spinners: Submerged Voices in Grimms' Fairy Tales," *New German Critique* 27 (Fall 1982): 146. "In terms of plot four sub-groups can be distinguished among the spinning tales. In the first, spinning itself is the subject of the tale. In the second, spinning functions as an indicator of the character or characteristics of the female protagonist; while in the third group, spinning symbolizes the female sex and/or onerous tasks." Bottigheimer argues that the submerged female voices of the tales indicate that women detested spinning. However, her argument overlooks the fact that women historically cherished spinning and that attitudes toward spinning underwent major shifts on the part of both men and women.

25. "Rumpelstiltskin's Bargain," 207-8.

26. Cf. Torborg Lundell, "Gender-Related Biases in the Type and Motif Indexes of Aarne and Thompson" in *Fairy Tales and Society: Illusion, Allusion, and Paradigm*, ed. Ruth B. Bottigheimer (Philadelphia: Univ. of Pennsylvania Press, 1986), 149-63.

3. BREAKING THE DISNEY SPELL

1. See Lewis Jacobs, "George Méliès: 'Artifically Arranged Scenes,'" in *The Emergence of Film Art: The Evolution and Development of the Motion Picture as an Art, from 1900 to the Present*, ed. Lewis Jacobs, 2nd Ed. (New York: Norton, 1979), 10-19.

2. *Ibid.*, 13.

3. (Cambridge: MIT Press, 1982), 11.

4. I am purposely using the word designer instead of animator because Disney was always designing things, made designs, and had designs. A designer is someone who indicates with a distinctive mark, and Disney put his mark on everything in his studios. A designing person is often a crafty person who manages to put his schemes into effect by hook or crook. Once Disney stopped animating, he became a designer.

5. "The Work of Art in the Age of Mechanical Reproduction" in *Illuminations,* trs. Harry Zohn (New York: Harcourt, Brace and World, 1968), 223.

6. See Leonard Mosley, *Disney's World* (New York: Stein and Day, 1985), 85-140.

7. *Disney's Art of Animation: From Mickey Mouse to Beauty and the Beast* (New York: Hyperion, 1991), 49.

8. See *The Woman Writer and the Nineteenth-Century Literary Imagination* (New Haven: Yale Univ. Press, 1979).

9. Cf. Charles Solomon, "Bad Girls Finish First in Memory of Disney Fans," *Milwaukee Journal,* TV Section (August 17, 1980): 28. This article cites the famous quote by Woody Allen in *Annie Hall:* "You know, even as a kid I always went for the wrong women. When my mother took me to see 'Snow White,' everyone fell in love with Snow White; I immediately fell for the Wicked Queen."

10. See Karen Merritt, "The Little Girl/Little Mother Transformation: The American Evolution of 'Snow White and the Seven Dwarfs,'" in *Storytelling in Animation: The Art of the Animated Image,* ed. John Canemaker (Los Angeles: American Film Institute, 1988), 105-21. Merritt makes the interesting point that

Disney's *Snow White* is an adaptation of a 1912 children's play (Disney saw it as a silent movie during his adolescence) still much performed today, written by a male Broadway producer under a female pseudonym; this play was an adaptation of a play for immigrant children from the tenements of lower East Side New York; and that play, in turn, was a translation and adaptation of a German play for children by a prolific writer of children's comedies and fairy tale drama. Behind these plays was the popularity of nineteenth and early twentieth century fairy tale pantomimes at Christmas in England and fairy tale plays in German and America. The imposition of childish behavior on the dwarves, Snow White's resulting mothering, the age ambiguities in both Snow White and the dwarves, the "Cinderella" elements, and the suppression of any form of sexuality were transmitted by that theatrical tradition, which embodied a thoroughly developed philosophy of moral education in representations for children. . . . By reading Disney's *Snow White* by the light of overt didacticism of his sources, he no longer appears the moral reactionary disdained by contemporary critics. Rather, he is the entertainer who elevates the subtext of play found in his sources and dares once again to frighten children (106).

Though it may be true that Disney was more influenced by an American theatrical and film tradition, the source of all these productions, one acknowledged by Disney, was the Grimms' tale. And, as I have argued, Disney was not particularly interested in experimenting with the narrative to shock children or provide a new perspective on the traditional story. For all intents and purposes his film reinforces the didactic messages of the Grimms' tale, and it is only in the technical innovations and designs that he did something startlingly new. It is not the object of critique to "disdain" or "condemn" Disney for reappropriating the Grimms' tradition to glorify the great designer but to understand those cultural and psychological forces that led him to map out his narrative strategies in fairy-tale animation.

111. *The Disney Version* (New York: Simon and Schuster, 1968), 227.

4. SPREADING MYTHS ABOUT IRON JOHN

1. It is interesting to compare the associations of the British reviewer, Martin Amis: "*Iron John* runs into trouble—into outright catastrophe—with the first word of its title. I don't know why I find this quite so funny (what's *wrong* with me?); I don't know why I still scream with laughter every time I think about it. Is it the spectacle of Bly's immediate self-defeat? Or is it because the title itself so firmly establishes the cultural impossibility of taking *Iron John* straight? Anyway, here's the difficulty; *iron* is rhyming slang for 'male homosexual'. Just as *ginger* (ginger beer) means 'queer', so, I'm afraid, *iron* (iron hoof) means 'poof'." "Return of the Male," *London Review of Books* 13 (December 5, 1991): 3.

2. *The Complete Fairy Tales of the Brothers Grimm*, trs. Jack Zipes (New York: Bantam, 1987), 488.

3. *Iron John: A Book About Men* (Reading, Massachusetts: Addison-Wesley, 1990), 6. All page references in my chapter refer to this book.

4. See my translation of this tale in *The Complete Fairy Tales of the Brothers Grimm* (New York: Bantam, 1987), 482-88.

5. *The Complete Fairy Tales of the Brothers Grimm*, 72.

6. *A Classification and Bibliography* (Helsinki: Suomalainen Tiedeakatemia, 1928), 53-4, 78.

7. Cf. Günter Dammann, "Goldener" in *Enzyklopädie des Märchens*, ed. Kurt Ranke, vol. 5 (Berlin: De Gruyter, 1987), 1372-1383, and Walter Scherf, "Der Eisenhans" in *Lexikon der Zaubermärchen* (Stuttgart: Kröner, 1982), 91-97.

8. I am basing this plot summary on *Robert der Teufel*. Reutlingen: Reutlinger Volksbücher, n.d. This version was probably published in 1900, and of course, there are numerous manuscripts and chapbooks that date back to the Middle Ages and were circulated up through the nineteenth century. The versions do not vary much. They tend to stress the "Christianization" of a pagan or demonic knight.

9. *Types of the Folk-Tale*, p. 53-54.

10. One of the more interesting versions that I recently uncovered is a French-Canadian tale entitled "Sir Goldenhair" in Marius Barbeau, *The Golden Phoenix and Other French-Canadian Fairy Tales*. Retold by Michael Hornyansky (New York: Walck, 1958). This delightful tale begins with a princess watching a new under-gardener named Petit Jean, who was always wearing an old-fashioned sheepskin wig and looking after his white horse. Of course, Petit Jean has golden hair and defeats the enemies of the kingdom with his white horse. In the end, the horse asks to be chopped in two as a reward for his services. He turns into a prince, and he and the head gardener marry the two sisters of the princess, who marries Petit Jean. There is no question here of a mentor. Rather, it is the horse who had been enchanted by a witch that provides the hero with the requisite help he needs.

11. The question of reception is always a complex one, and obviously Bly would like to have his book transcend America. There are statements in the book that indicate that he feels he is speaking about eternal maleness. However, the reception in England has been lukewarm, and there is something characteristically "American" about his book that is frightening: its imperial naiveté and/or its naive imperialism.

12. "Return of the Male," *London Review of Books* 13 (December 5, 1991): 3.

13. Cf. Mark Lawson, "The 'Wild Man' Mystique" *World Press Review* (December 1991): 40, and Diane Johnson, "Something New for the Boys," *New York Review of Books* 39 (January 16, 1992): 13-17.

14. Cf. Susan Faludi, *Backlash: The Undeclared War Against American Women* (New York: Crown, 1991), and Naomi Wolf, *The Beauty Myth: How Images of Beauty Are Used Against Women* (New York: Morrow, 1991).

15. "Why Iron John is No Gift to Women," *New York Times Book Review* (February 23, 1992): 33.

16. "'Enemy of the Mother': A Feminist Response to the Men's Movement," *Ms.* 2 (March/April, 1992): 82.

17. "Captain Bly," *The Nation* 253 (September 9, 1991): 270.

18. Cf. Kim Ode, "Robert Bly: A Man's Man Rethinks his Role," *Star Tribune Magazine* (February 2, 1992): 4-11.

19. Ode, "A Man's Man Rethinks his Role," 5.

20. *Mythologies*, trs. Annette Lavers (London: Granada, 1973), 142-43.

5. OZ AS AMERICAN MYTH

1. See Aljean Harmetz, *The Making of the Wizard of Oz* (New York: Knopf, 1978).

2. (Albany: State University of New York Press, 1991).

3. *Ibid.*, 229-30.

4. *The Wizard of Oz: The Screenplay*, 39-40.

5. *Ibid.*, 132.

6. "Kark Marx and Humanity: The Material of Hope," in *On Karl Marx*, trs. John Maxwell (New York: Seabury, 1971), 30-31.

7. *A Barnstormer in Oz* (New York: Berkley Books, 1982), 23.

8. *Ibid.*, 160.

9. *Was* (New York: Knopf, 1992), 364.

10. *Ibid.*, 368-69.

6. CONTEMPORARY AMERICAN FAIRY TALE

1. *Die Zaubergärten der Phantasie: Zur Theorie und Geschichte des Kunstmärchens* (Heidelberg: Carl Winter Universitätsverlag, 1978), 272-73.

2. "On Fairy Tales," in *European Literary Theory and Practice*, ed. Vernon W. Gras (New York: Delta, 1973), 352.

3. Cf. Jack Zipes, ed., *Don't Bet on the Prince: Contemporary Fairy Tales in North America and Canada* (New York: Methuen, 1986).

4. Typically, when the producers of a fairy-tale play or film believe that it will be a success, they will publish a book simultaneously with the production. In this case, the book is Stephen Sondheim and James Lapine, *Into the Woods*, adapt. and illustr. Hudson Talbott (New York: Crown, 1988).

5. For an interesting discussion of feminist versions in North America, Great Britain, and Australia, see Bronwyn Davies, *Frogs and Snails and Feminist Tales: Preschool Children and Gender* (Sydney: Allen and Unwin, 1989).

6. Babette Cole, who has also written *Prince Cinders* (1987), is British, but as in the case of some other authors such as the Canadian Robert Munsch, who wrote *The Paper Bag Princess* (1980), her works are widely distributed in the United States.

7. Two other trite and melodramatic novels based on the TV series have appeared since the publication of the first one. See Barbara Hambly, *Beauty and the Beast: Song of Orpheus* (New York: Avon, 1990) and Ru Emerson, *Beauty and the Beast: Masques* (New York; Avon, 1990). In addition, one can purchase six videotapes of the TV series that contain the most crucial episodes.

8. *Beauty and the Beast* (New York: Avon, 1989), 242.

9. *The Princess Bride* (New York: Ballantine, 1987), 283.

10. *Tam Lin* (New York: Tor, 1991), 461.

11. *Dragonfield and Other Stories* (London: Futura, 1988), xi.

12. *Ibid.*, 203.

13. *Ibid.*, 32.

14. *Ibid.*, 45.

15. "Folk and Literary Narrative in a Postmodern Context: The Case of the *Märchen*," *Fabula* 29 (1989): 1.

16. *Ibid.*, 3.

17. *Pricksongs and Descants* (New York: Dutton, 1970), 61.

18. *Ibid.*, 63.

19. *Ibid.*, 65.

20. Davenport is an independent filmmaker, who has made 10 films based on fairy tales and folk tales and given them Appalachian settings. His screenplays and interpretations of the tales are original, and he is constantly experimenting with providing new perspectives on viewing American society through film adaptations of fairy tales. See Tom Davenport and Gary Carden, *From the Brothers Grimm: A Contemporary Retelling of American Folktales and Classic Stories* (Fort Atkinson, Wisconsin: Highsmith, 1992).

21. This volume contains tales by Terry Brooks, Katherine Kurtz, Lawrence Watt-Evans, Susan Dexter, Wayland Drew, Barbara Hambly, Isaac Asimov, C.J. Cherryh, Anne McCaffrey, and Lester Del Rey himself. For an excellent critique of this volume, see Mike Ashley, "Once Upon a Time," *Million* (March-April, 1992): 53-55.

BIBLIOGRAPHY

PRIMARY SOURCES

Attic Press. *Rapunzel's Revenge*. Dublin: Attic Press, 1985.
————. *Ms Muffet and Others*. Dublin: Attic Press, 1986.
————. *Mad and Bad Fairies*. Dublin: Attic Press, 1987.
————. *Sweeping Beauties*. Dublin: Attic Press, 1989.
Anthony, Edward and Joseph. *The Fairies Up-to-Date*. London: Thornton Butterworth, c. 1920.
Auerbach, Nina and U.C. Knoepflmacher, eds. *Forbidden Journeys: Fairy Tales and Fantasies by Victorian Women Writers*. Chicago: University of Chicago Press, 1992.
Banks, Lynne Reid. *The Farthest-Away Mountain*. New York: Doubleday, 1976.
Barbeau, Marius. *The Golden Phoenix and Other French Canadian Fairy Tales*. Retold by Michael Hornyansky. New York: Walck, 1958.
Barthelme, Donald. *Snow White*. New York: Atheneum, 1967.
Baum, L. Frank. *The Wonderful Wizard of Oz*. Ed. Martin Gardner. Illustr. W.W. Denslow. New York: Dover, 1960. (Based on the original text of 1900 published by George M. Hill in Chicago.)
Beauty and the Beast and Other Fairy Tales. Illustr. Rene Cloke. New York: Gallery Books, 1990.
Brett, Jan. *Beauty and the Beast*. New York: Clarion Books, 1989.
Broumas, Olga. *Beginning with O*. New Haven: Yale University Press, 1977.
Brust, Steven. *The Sun, the Moon, and the Stars*. New York: Ace Books, 1987.

Calmenson, Stephanie. *The Principal's New Clothes.* Illustr. Denise Brunkus. New York: Scholastic, 1989.

Carryl, Guy Wetmore. *Grimm Tales Made Gay.* Boston: Houghton, Mifflin and Co., 1902.

Carter, Angela. *The Bloody Chamber and Other Stories.* London: Gollancz, 1979.

Carter, Angela, ed. *The Virago Book of Fairy Tales.* London: Virago, 1990.

Cole, Babette. *Princess Smarty Pants.* New York: G.P. Putnam's Sons, 1986.

———. *Prince Cinders.* New York: G.P. Putnam's Sons, 1987.

Coover, Robert. *Pricksongs and Descants.* New York: Dutton, 1970.

———. *Pinocchio in Venice.* New York: Simon and Schuster, 1991.

Crane, Walter. *Beauty and the Beast.* London: Routledge, 1875.

Dahl, Roald. *Revolting Rhymes.* London: Jonathan Cape, 1982.

Dalkey, Kara. *The Nightingale.* New York: Ace Books, 1988.

Datlow, Ellen, and Terri Windling. *Snow White, Blood Red.* New York: William Morrow, 1993.

Davenport, Tom and Gary Carden. *From the Brothers Grimm. A Contemporary Retelling of American Folktales and Classic Stories.* Fort Atkinson, Wisconsin: Highsmith, 1992.

Davis, Gwen. *The Princess and the Pauper.* Boston: Little, Brown and Company, 1989.

Dean, Pamela. *Tam Lin.* New York: Tor, 1991.

Del Rey, Lester and Risa Kessler. *Once Upon a Time: A Treasury of Modern Fairy Tales.* New York: Ballantine, 1991.

Disney's Beauty and the Beast. New York: W.H. Smith, 1991.

Emerson, Ru. *Beauty and the Beast: Masques.* New York: Avon, 1990.

Ende, Michael. *Neverending Story.* New York: Penguin, 1984.

Farmer, Philip José. *A Barnstormer in Oz.* New York: Berkeley, 1982.

Feist, Raymond E. *Faerie Tale.* New York: Doubleday, 1988.

Gearhart, Sally Miller. "Roja and Leopold" in *And A Deer's Ear, Eagle's Song and Bear's Grace: Animals and Women,* Eds. Theresa Corrigan and Stephanie Hoppe. Pittsburgh: Cleis, 1990.

Goldman, William. *The Princess Bride.* New York: Ballantine Books, 1974.

Hambly, Barbara. *Beauty and the Beast.* New York: Avon, 1989.

———. *Beauty and the Beast: Song of Orpheus.* New York: Avon. 1990.

Hartwell, David G., ed. *Masterpieces of Fantasy and Enchantment.* New York: St. Martin's Press, 1988.

Hay, Sara Henderson. *Story Hour.* Garden City: Doubleday, 1963.

Heriz, Patrick de. *Fairy Tales with a Twist.* London: Peter Lunn, 1946.

Holeinone, Peter. *The Story of Little Red Riding Hood and Other Tales.* Illustr. Piero Cattaneo. New York: Gallery Books, 1990.

Hyman, Trina Schart. *Little Red Riding Hood.* New York: Holiday House, 1983.

Janosch. *Not Quite as Grimm.* London: Abelard-Schuman, 1974.

Kramer, Rita. "Rumpelstiltskin: His Story." *South Dakota Review* 25 (Sumer, 1987): 78-81.

Kushner, Ellen. *Swordspoint.* New York: Tor Books, 1987.

Lamb, Charles. *Beauty and the Beast.* Ed. Andrew Lang. London: Leadenhall Press, 1886.

Lang, Andrew. *Blue Fairy Book.* London: Longmans, Green and Co., 1889.

Langley, Noel, Florence Ryerson, and Edgar Allan Woolf. *The Wizard of Oz: The Screenplay.* Ed. Michael Patrick Hearn. New York: Delta, 1989.

Lee, Tanith. *Red as Blood, or Tales of the Sisters Grimmer.* New York: DAW, 1983.

L'Héritier, Marie-Jeanne. *La Tour Ténebreuse et Les Jours lumineux.* Paris: Barbin, 1705.

Lint, Charles de. *Jack The Giant Killer.* New York: Ace Books, 1987.

Lurie, Alison, ed. *Clever Gretchen and Other Forgotten Tales.* New York: Corwell, 1980.

Mahy, Margaret. *The Changeover.* New York: Scholastic, 1974.

Marshall, James. *Red Riding Hood.* New York: Dial, 1987.

Mayer, Mercer. *Herbert the Timid Dragon.* New York: Golden Press, 1980.

McKinley, Robin. *Beauty: A Retelling of the Story of Beauty and the Beast.* New York: Harper and Row, 1978.

Minard, Rosemary, Ed. *Womenfolk and Fairy Tales.* Boston: Houghton Mifflin, 1975.

Morgan, Robin. *The Mer-Child: A Legend for Children and Other Adults.* Illustr. Jesse Spicer Zerner. New York: The Feminist Press, 1991.

Munsch, Robert. *The Paper Bag Princess.* Illustr. M. Marchenko. Toronto: Annick Press, 1980.

Naubert, Benedikte. "The Cloak." Trs. Jeannine Blackwell in: *Bitter Healing: German Women Writers from 1700 to 1830*. Eds. Jeannine Blackwell and Suzanne Zantop. Lincoln: University of Nebraska Press, 1990. pp. 201-78.

Perrault, Charles. *Little Red Riding Hood*. Illustr. Sarah Moon. Mankato, Minnesota: Creative Education, 1983.

Phelps, Ethel Johnston, ed. *Tatterhood and Other Tales*. Old Westbury, New York: Feminist Press, 1978.

———, ed. *The Maid of the North: Feminist Folk Tales from around the World*. New York: Holt, Rinehart and Winston, 1981.

Philip, Neil, ed. *The Cinderella Story*. London: Penguin, 1989.

Pogrebin, Letty Cottin, ed. *Stories for Free Children*. New York: McGraw-Hill, 1982.

Quiller-Couch, Sir Arthur. *The Sleeping Beauty and Other Tales from the Old French*. Illustr. Edmund Dulac. London: Hodder and Stoughton, 1910.

Redgrove, Peter. *The One Who Set Out to Study Fear*. London: Bloomsbury, 1989.

Robert der Teufel. Reutlingen: Reutlinger Volksbücher, n.d. (c. 1900).

Rowland, Della. *Beauty and the Beast*. Illustr. Babara Lanza. Chicago: Contemporary Books, 1990.

Rudd, Elizabeth. *Beauty and the Beast*. Illustr. Eleanor Vere Boyle. New York: Barron's Educational Series, 1988.

Rushdie, Salman. *Haroun and the Sea of Stories*. New York: Viking, 1990.

Ryman, Geoff. *Was*. New York: Knopf, 1992.

Scieszka, Jon. *The Frog Prince Continued*. New York: Viking, 1991.

Scieszka, Jon, and Lane Smith. *The Stinky Cheese and Other Fairly Stupid Tales*. New York: Viking, 1992.

Sendak, Maurice, *Dear Mili*. Trs. Ralph Manheim. New York: Farrar, Straus and Giroux, 1988.

Sexton, Anne. *Transformations*. Boston: Houghton Mifflin, 1971.

Smith, Albert. *Beauty and the Beast*. Illustr. Alfred Croquill. London: Orr, 1853.

Shwartz, Susan, ed. *Hecate's Cauldron*. New York: Daw Books, 1982.

Snow White and the Seven Dwarfs. Illustr. Dorothea King. Newmarket: England: Brimax Books, 1990.

Sondheim, Stephen and James Lapine. *Into the Woods*. Adapt. and Illustr. Hudson Talbott. New York: Crown, 1988.

Strauss, Gwen. *Trail of Stones*. London: Julia MacRae Books, 1990.

Tigerman, Tracy and Margaret McCurry. *Dorothy in Dreamland.*
Illustr. Stanley Tigerman. New York: Rizzoli, 1991.

Volkov, Alexander. *Tales of Magic Land 1: The Wizard of the Emer-
ald City and Urfin Jus and his Wooden Soldiers.* Trs. Peter L.
Blystone. Staten Island: Red Branch Press, 1991.

Waddell, Martin. *The Tough Princess.* Illustr. Patrick Benson. New
York: Philomel Books, 1986.

Walker, Wendy. *The Sea-Rabbit Or, The Artist of Life.* Los Angeles:
Sun and Moon Press, 1988.

Wells, Joel. *Grim Fairy Tales for Adults.* New York: Macmillan,
1967.

Wrede, Patricia C. *Snow White and Rose Red.* New York: Tor Books,
1989.

Yep, Laurence. *The Rainbow People.* New York: Harper Collins,
1989.

Yolen, Jane, *Tales of Wonder.* New York: Schocken, 1983.

———. *Dragonfield and Other Stories.* New York: Ace Books, 1985.

———. *Briar Rose.* New York: Tor Books, 1992.

Zipes, Jack, ed. *Don't Bet on the Prince: Contemporary Feminist
Fairy Tales in North America and England.* New York: Methuen,
1986.

———, ed. *Beauties, Beasts, and Enchantment: French Classical
Fairy Tales.* New York: New American Library, 1989.

———, trs. *The Complete Fairy Tales of the Brothers Grimm.* New
York Bantam, 1987.

———, ed. *Spells of Enchantment: The Wondrous Fairy Tales of
Western Culture.* New York: Viking, 1991.

SECONDARY SOURCES

Aarne, Antti, and Stith Thompson. *The Types of the Folk-Tale: A
Classification and Bibliography.* F.F. Communications NO. 74.
Helsinki: Suomalainen Tiedeakatemia, 1928.

Alvey, R. Gerald. "Eisen, eisern" in *Enzyklopädie des Märchens.* Ed.
Kurt Ranke. vol. 3. Berlin: De Gruyter, 1981.

Amis, Martin. "Return of the Male." *London Review of Books* 13
(December 5, 1991): 3-5.

Apel, Friedmar. *Die Zaubergärten der Phantasie: Zur Theorie und
Geschichte des Kunstmärchens.* Heidelberg: Winter, 1978.

Ariès, Philippe. "At the Point of Origin." *Yale French Studies* 43
(1969): 15-23.

Baader, Renate. *Dames de Lettres: Autorinnen des preziösen, hochar-istokratischen und 'modernen' Salons (1649-1698): Mlle de Scu-déry—Mlle de Montpensieer—Mme d'Aulnoy.* Stuttgart: Metzler, 1986.

Bacchilega, Cristina. "Folk and Literary Narrative in a Postmodern Context: The Case of the Märchen." *Fabula* 29 (1989): 302-16.

Baines, Patricia. *Spinning Wheels, Spinners and Spinning.* London: Batsford, 1977.

Barchilon, Jacques. *Le conte merveilleux français de 1690 à 1790.* Paris: Champion, 1975.

Barthes, Roland. *Mythologies.* Trs. Annette Lavers. London: Granada, 1973.

———. *Image—Music—Text.* New York: Hill and Wang: 1971.

Beit, Hedwig. *Symbolik des Märchens: Gegensatz und Erneurung im Märchen.* Vol. 2. 2nd Ed. Bern: 1965.

Bendazzi, Giannalberto. *Le Film d'Animation.* Trs. Genviève Vidal. Grenoble: La Pensée Sauvage, 1985.

Benjamin, Jessica. *The Bonds of Love: Psychoanalysis, Feminism, and the Problem of Domination.* New York: Pantheon, 1988.

Benjamin, Walter. *Illuminations.* Trs. Harry Zohn. New York: Harcourt, Brace and World, 1968.

Bergler, Edmund. "The Clinical Importance of 'Rumpelstiltskin' as Anti-Male Manifesto." *American Imago* 18 (1961): 65-70.

"The Big Bad Wolf." *Fortune* X (November 1934): 88-95, 142-48.

Blackwell, Jeannine and Suzanne Zantop. *Bitter Healing: German Women Writers 1700-1830 from 1700 to 1830.* Lincoln: University of Nebraska Press, 1990.

Bloch, Ernst. *On Karl Marx.* Trs. John Maxwell. New York: Seabury, 1971.

Bly, Robert. *Iron John: A Book About Men.* Reading, Massachusetts: Addison-Wesley, 1990.

Bolte, Johannes, and Georg Polivka. "Der Eisenhans" in *Anmerkungen zu den Kinder- und Hausmärchen.* Vol. 3. Leipzig: Dieterich, 1918. Pp. 94-114.

Bottigheimer, Ruth B. "Tale Spinners: Submerged Voices in Grimms' Fairy Tales." *New German Critique* 27 (1982): 141-50.

Brooks, Peter. "Toward Supreme Fictions." *Yale French Studies* 43 (1969): 5-14.

Bryant, Sylvia. "Re-Constructing Oedipus Through 'Beauty and the Beast.'" *Criticism* 31 (Fall, 1989): 439-53.

Bühler, Charlotte, and Josephine Bilz. *Das Märchen und die Phantasie des Kindes*. Munich: Nymphenburger Verlag, 1958.

Bürger, Peter. *Theory of the Avant-Garde*. Trs. Michael Shaw. Minneapolis: University of Minnesota Press, 1984.

Butor, Michel. "On Fairy Tales." In *European Literary Theory and Practice*. Ed. Vernon W. Gras. New York: Delta, 1973. Pp. 351-56.

Canemaker, John, ed. *Storytelling in Animation: The Art of the Animated Image*. Los Angeles: The American Film Institute, 1988.

Clancy, Patricia. "A French Writer and Educator in England: Mme Le Prince de Beaumont." *Studies on Voltaire and the Eighteenth Century*. 201 (1982): 195-208.

Clodd, Edward. *Tim Tit Tot: An Essay of Savage Philosphy*. London: Duckworth, 1898.

Crafton, Donald. *Before Mickey: The Animated Film 1898-1928*. Cambridge: MIT Press, 1982.

Dammann, Günter. "Goldener" in *Enzyklopädie des Märchens*. Ed. Kurt Ranke. vol. 5. Berlin: De Gruyter, 1987. 1371-83.

Davies, Bronwyn. *Frogs and Snails and Feminist Tales: Preschool Children and Gender*. Sydney: Allen and Unwin, 1989.

Davis, Natalie Zemon. "Women in the Crafts in Sixteenth-Century Lyon." *Feminist Studies* 8 (1982): 46-80.

Doubiago, Sharon. "'Enemy of the Mother': A Feminist Response to the Men's Movement." *Ms.* 2 (March/April, 1992): 82-5.

Eliade, Mircea. *Myth and Reality*. Trs. Willard R. Trask. New York: Harper and Row, 1963.

Elias, Norbert. *The Civilizing Process: The History of Manners*. New York: Urizen, 1978.

Faludi, Susan. *The Backlash: The Undeclared War Against American Women*. New York: Crown, 1991.

Fink, Gonthier Louis. "Les avatars de Rumpelstilzchen. La vie d'un conte populaire." In *Deutsche-Französisches Gespräch im Lichte der Märchen*, ed. Ernst Kracht. Münster: Aschendorff, 1964. Pp. 46-72.

Freud, Sigmund. *Civilization and Its Discontents*. (1930) vol. 21. London: Hogarth, 1953.

Gilbert, Sandra, and Susan Gubar. *The Madwoman in the Attic: The Woman Writer and the Nineteenth-Century Literary Imagination*. New Haven: Yale University Press, 1979.

Gillot, Hubert. *La Querelle des Anciens et des Modernes*. Geneva: Slatkine, 1968. Reprint of 1914 edition.

Gingold, Alfred. *Fire in the John: The Manly Man in the Age of Sissification*. New York: St. Martin's Press, 1991.

Grimm, Jacob, and Wilhelm. *Kinder- und Hausmärchen*. Ed. Heinz Rölleke. 3 vols. Stuttgart: Reclam, 1980.

Gunn, Eileen, and Kathleen Ann Goonan, "There's No Place Like Home: Two Takes on Geoff Ryman's *Was*." *The New York Review of Science Fiction* 51 (November, 1992): 1, 10-13.

Halas, John, and Roger Manvell. *Design in Motion*. New York: Visual Communications Books—Hastings House, 1962.

Harmetz, Haljean. *The Making of the Wizard of Oz*. New York: Knopf, 1978.

Hearne, Betsy. *Beauty and the Beast: Visions and Revisions of an Old Tale*. Chicago: University of Chicago Press, 1989.

Horkheimer, Max, and Theodor W. Adorno. *Dialectic of Enlightenment*. Trs. John Cumming. New York: Seabury, 1969.

Jacobs, Lewis. *Introduction to the Art of the Movies*. New York: Noonday, 1962.

———, ed. *The Emergence of Film Art: The Evolution and Development of the Motion Picture as an art from 1900 to the Present*. 2nd Edition. New York: Norton, 1979.

Johnson, Diane. "Something for the Boys." *New York Review of Books* 39 (January 16, 1992): 13-17.

Johnston, Jill. "Why Iron John Is No Gift to Women," *The New York Times Book Review* (February 23, 1992): 1, 28, 31, 33-4.

Kahn, Otto. "Rumpelstilz hat wirklich gelebt." *Rheinisches Jahrbuch für Volkskunde* 17/18 (1966/67): 143-84.

Katz, Leo. "The Rumpelstiltskin Complex." *Contemporary Psychoanalysis* 10 (1974): 117-24.

Knight, Arthur. *The Liveliest Art*. New York: Macmillan, 1957.

Lawson, Mark. "The 'Wild Man' Mystique." *World Press Review* (December 1991): 40.

Lüthi, Max. "Rumpelstilzchen." *Anataios* 12 (1971): 419-36.

Lundell, Torborg. "Gender-Related Biases in the Type and Motif Indexes of Aarne and Thompson." In *Fairy Tales and Society: Illusion, Allusion, and Paradigm*, ed. Ruth B. Bottigheimer, Philadelphia: University of Pennsylvania Press, 1986. Pp. 149-63.

Mackensen, Lutz, ed. "Goldener" in *Handwörterbuch des deutschen Märchens*. vol. 2. Berlin: De Gruyter, 1934/40. 648-51.

Marshall, Howard Wright. "'Tom Tit Tot': A Comparative Essay on Aarne-Thompson Type 500—The Name of the Helper." *Folklore* 84 (1973): 51-57.

Matlin, Leonard. *Of Mice and Magic: A History of American Animated Cartoons.* New York: NAL, 1980.

Medick, Hans. "Village Spinning Bees: Sexual Culture and Free Time among Rural Youth in Early Modern Germany." In H. Medick and D. Sabean, eds. *Interest and Emotion: Essays on the Study of Family and Kinship.* Cambridge: Cambridge University Press, 1984. Pp. 317-40.

Medick, Hans and David Warren Sabean. *Interest and Emotion: Essays on the Study of Family and Kinship.* Cambridge: Cambridge University Press, 1984.

Merritt, "The Little Girl/Little Mother Transformation: The American Evolution of 'Snow White and the Seven Dwarfs.'" in *Storytelling in Animation: The Art of the Animated Image.* Ed. John Canemaker. Los Angeles: The American Film Institute, 1988. Pp. 105-21.

Miller, Martin. "Poor Rumpelstiltskin." *Psychoanalytic Quarterly* 54 (1985): 73-6.

Mosely, Leonard. *Disney's World.* New York: Stein and Day, 1985.

"Mouse and Man." *Time* XXX (December 27, 1937): 19-21.

Nathanson, Paul. *Over the Rainbow: The Wizard of Oz As a Secular Myth.* Albany: State University of New York Press, 1991.

Ode, Kim. "Robert Bly: A Man's Man Rethinks his Role." *Star Tribune Magazine* (February 2, 1992): 4-11.

Perrault, Charles. *Memoirs of My Life.* Ed. and Trs. Jeanne Morgan Zarucchi. Columbia: University of Missouri Press, 1989.

Reckford, Kenneth. "Allegiance to Utopia." *The Baum Bugle* 32 (Winter 1988): 11-13.

Rinsley, Donald B. and Elizabeth Bergmann. "Enchantment and Alchemy: The Story of Rumpelstiltskin." *Bulletin of the Menninger Clinic* 47 (1983): 1-14.

Robert, Raymonde. *Le conte de fées littéraire en France de la fin du XVIIe à la fin du XVIIIe siècle.* Nancy: Presses Universitaires de Nancy, 1981.

Röhrich, Lutz. "Rumpelstilzchen. Vom Methodenpluralismus in der Erzählforschung." In *Sage und Märchen. Erzählforschung heute.* Freiburg: Herder, 1976. Pp. 272-91.

Rölleke, Heinz, Ed. *Die älteste Märchensammlung der Brüder Grimm.* Cologny-Geneva: Fondation Martin Bodmer, 1975.

Roheim, Géza. "Tim, Tit, Tot." *Psychoanalytic Review* 36 (1949): 365-69.

Rowe, Karen E. "To Spin a Yarn: The Female Voice in Folklore and

Fairy Tale." In *Fairy Tales and Society: Illusion, Allusion, and Paradigm*, ed. Ruth B. Bottigheimer, Philadelphia: University of Pennsylvania Press, 1986.

Rowley, Julius L. "Rumpelstilzkin in the Analytical Situation." *International Journal of Psycho-Analysis* 32 (1951): 190-95.

Rumpf, Marianne. "Spinnerinnen und Spinnen: Märchendeutung aus kulturhistorischer Sicht." In *Die Frau im Märchen*, eds. Sigrid Früh und Rainer Wehse. Kassel: Erich Röth, 1985. Pp. 59-72.

———. "Spinnstubenfrauen, Kinderschreckgestalten und Frau Perchta." *Fabula* 17 (1976): 215-42.

Rushdie, Salman. *The Wizard of Oz*. London: British Film Institute, 1992.

Scherf, Walter. *Lexikon der Zäubermärchen*. Stuttgart: Kröner, 1982.

Schickel, Richard. *The Disney Version: The Life, Times, Art and Commerce of Walt Disney*. New York: Simon and Schuster, 1968.

Schneider, Jane. "Rumpelstiltskin's Bargain: Folklore and the Merchant Capitalist Intensification of Linen Manufacture in Early Modern Europe." In *Cloth and Human Experience*, Eds. Annette B. Weiner and Jane Schneider. Washington D.C.: Smithsonian Institution Press, 1989. Pp. 177-213.

Schuurman, C.J. 1950. "The Psychoanalytical and the Psychosocial Interpretation of Fairy Tales." *Folia Psychiatrica* 53 (1950): 509-18.

Solomon, Charles. "Bad Girls Finish First in Memory of Disney Fans." *Milwaukee Journal*, Television Section (August 17, 1980): 28.

———, ed. *The Art of the Animated Image*. Los Angeles: The American Film Institute, 1987.

Solotaroff, Ted. "Captain Bly." *The Nation* 253 (September 9, 1991): 270-74.

Steinlein, Rüdiger. *Die domestizierte Phantasie: Studien zur Kinderliteratur, Kinderlektüre und Literaturpädagogik des 18. und frühen 19. Jahrhunderts*. Heidelberg: Winter, 1987.

Thomas, Bob. *Disney's Art of Animation: From Mickey Mouse to Beauty and the Beast*. New York: Hyperion, 1991.

Treusch-Dieter, Gerburg. *Wie den Frauen der Faden aus der Hand genommen wurde: Die Spindel der Notwendigkeit*. Berlin: Ästhetik und Kommunikation, 1983.

Velay-Vallantin, Catherine. *L'Histoire des contes*. Paris: Fayard, 1992.

Vidal, Gore. "The Wizard of the 'Wizard.'" *The New York Review of Books* 24 (September 29, 1977): 10-15; "On Rereading the Oz Books." *The New York Review of Books* 24 (October 13, 1977): 38-42.

Weigle, Marta. *Spiders and Spinsters: Woman and Mythology.* Albuquerque: University of New Mexico Press, 1982.

Weiner, Annette B. and Jane Schneider, Eds. *Cloth and Human Experience.* Washington D.C.: Smithsonian Institution Press, 1989.

Wolf, Naomi. *The Beauty Myth: How Images of Beauty Are Used
Against Women.* New York: Morrow, 1991.

Zipes, Jack. *Fairy Tales and the Art of Subversion.* London: Heinemann, 1983.

————. "The Rise of the French Fairy Tale and the Decline of France"
in *Beauties, Beasts and Enchantment: Classic French Fairy Tales.*
Trs. Jack Zipes. New York: NAL, 1989. Pp. 1-15.

————. *The Trials and Tribulations of Little Red Riding Hood.* Rev.
Ed. New York: Routledge, 1993.

INDEX